Conversation on Networking:

finding, developing, and maintaining relationships for business and life.

Kay Keenan
Steven Smolinsky

published by
Forever Talking Press

Copyright © 2006

Kay Keenan and Steven Smolinsky

Forever Talking Press

Birchrunville, Pennsylvania, 19421

Printed in the United States of America by Bentley Graphic Communications

Library of Congress Number: 2006921258

ISBN 0-9776945-051995

Conversation On Networking®
is a registered trademark of Kay Keenan and Steven Smolinsky.

Comments to:
KayandSteve@ConversationOnNetworking.com

IDEAS TO PONDER

Tip of the Page

Networking is not a zero sum game... the whole is definitely greater than the sum of the parts.

THANKS:

Writing this preface is the most amazing experience. *The Book* is done.... well, almost. There's still some final editing and design but there's really going to be... *Conversation on Networking: The Book*. Actually, we guess that by the time you are reading this we really will be done and you'll be holding... *The Book*.

Of course, Steve and Kay have been traveling around presenting *The Show* and writing this book. But it all happened due to serendipity. As we say, plan to be ready to take advantage of random opportunities. So we want to start this book by thanking our mid-wife, Howard Weisz, President of HW Associates. Howard brought us together for our initial *Conversation* at a Mid-Atlantic Consultants breakfast, and he has been a strong supporter ever since.

Early on we presented several public seminars. Yup, we actually rented space, provided breakfast, and hawked *The Show*. We expanded our girth for these by inviting Joel Smith and Barry Meyers, Principals of The People Source Group to join us. They provided us with new ideas and organization and they helped us get the word out that we existed. We thank them for this help and support as we found our sea legs.

But as is the way with waistlines, we eventually dieted back down to fit our original clothes. It just felt right.

And our groupies, and even those who've only seen us once, what can I say? Thank you, thank you, and thank you. You've given us energy, inspiration, stories, wisdom, advice, laughs, and even some aggravation. Not to mention inviting us to some nice places and helping pay the rent. Special thanks to our families for some of the stories that appear in the book. We have not protected your identities so we hope we haven't embarrassed you too badly.

Tip of the Page

Life, and networking, should be fun. Enjoy yourself!

As you read this, think about Anita Janney, our most wonderful friend and designer. The reason this is so visually stimulating is totally due to her exceptional eye for design and hand for illustrations. And we even want to thank Steve's neighbor Evan Emery. Young Evan, he's still in high school as we write this, was nice enough to do a few illustrations under Anita's guidance.

If you find anything needing correction or change send it to us but don't blame Anita or our proofreaders – we didn't accept all their changes. And while we're talking about sending us stuff... stories, comments, thoughts are always welcome at KayandSteve@ConversationOnNetworking.com.

And finally, you, our readers. Have fun. Enjoy the stories. Do the exercises. Practice. And have fun. And thanks. And remember... this book makes a great present for graduations, birthdays, anniversaries, Valentine's Day, Halloween, and even leveling the legs of restaurant tables.

Thanks.

Kay Keenan   Steven Smolinsky

INTRODUCTION ~ IT'S PERSONAL

As we wrote this book we began to notice some interesting things. This seems to be one of the rewards of being a writer... the opportunity to find out what's been floating around in your head looking for an outlet. We noticed that we really do think about networking differently than most people. Hence, the answer to the question I'm sure you asked yourself, "Why another book on networking?"

One of the things we focus on is personal choice. Personal choice is the art of finding your own style. It's what works best for you. We believe there is no one right answer. The right answer for you is what works for you, what you're comfortable doing and saying. So instead of giving you prescriptive answers we've tried to give you ideas to try out. Keep this in mind as you read and do the exercises.

There is no right answer to most of the issues we discuss. There is however, a wrong answer... do nothing. This makes it pretty simple to improve your skills... do something – anything. Really. Almost anything you do to improve your networking skills is better than ignoring the need to develop and maintain relationships.

So your first choice, after buying (hopefully... if you've borrowed this book feel free to send us a few dollars after realizing how we've improved your skills) this book is to decide whether to read this introduction now and be forewarned about some things, or to wait and read it at the end and see if you pick up the themes we're going to touch on. It's your choice.

One of the things we realized while writing this book is that networking is work. It should be fun and exciting and entertaining and rewarding, but it's still work. And to be successful at relationship building requires knowledge and planning and practice. This book is full of exercises, activities, and things for you to do to grow your confidence and expertise. Do the activities, or make up your own. If you practice as you read, we're pretty sure you'll become a more successful networker. (We wanted to guarantee this but our attorneys got involved).

The first theme we've already mentioned, personal choice. You each have a different background, education, behavioral style, age, sex, and ethnicity. And even if two of you happen to share all of these characteristics, you've integrated them differently. Even identical twins have some differences. So how dumb would we be to suggest that we have the single answer for all of you. We've been called dumb, but never that dumb. So there are no magic bullets or lists of must dos. Rather, we hope to get you thinking, give you some ideas to play with, and suggest some exercises to get the old synapses sparking. Ideally, you'll use this process to develop your very own method for developing and maintaining great relationships and connections.

A second theme turns out to be planning.

There's no excuse for being unprepared when you meet someone. And we mean anytime you meet someone, from a formal business event to just sitting next to someone at your kid's third grade play. Throughout this book we've suggested many ways to prepare to meet people. Try them out and keep the ones that work for you.

The third theme is practice.

It doesn't matter what great knowledge is stored in your head if you can't use it when required. As we've all heard, "practice makes perfect." Or maybe, "the more I practice the luckier I get." Try out the ideas we've presented. Keep the ones you like. Do the exercises. Make up your own ways to practice. When your family and friends can't stand you practicing on them anymore, go to a distant city and practice on strangers.

Our fourth theme is flexibility.

Flexibility allows you to pick what works for you. Flexibility allows you to say different things in different situations or with different people. Flexibility also allows you to adapt to the situation. We haven't done any scientific studies about this, but we're convinced that the flexibility you learn about networking will help you out in all you do.

And finally... have fun.

Although we said above that there's work in this book, it's not work you need to force yourself to do. It's enjoyable work. You're going to be learning how to be more effective and successful at meeting people, developing relationships, and finding new friends. Sounds like fun to us. So don't take yourself or us too seriously. Play around with our ideas and suggestions. Discuss them with your friends. Adapt and modify as useful. Have a good time.

One Last Note: As you noticed on the cover, this book was written by two people, Kay Keenan and Steven Smolinsky. We're really different. Some people might even say we are the yin and the yang. One of the reasons we have fun doing our show *Conversation On Networking* is that we can argue and disagree and offer different ideas to our audience/participants. As you can imagine, writing this book was an interesting exercise in who gets the last word. So we flip back and forth between using "I" and "we." Some places one or the other of us has clearly mentioned whose ideas are being expressed. Some places, it's not specified. Have fun figuring it out and be flexible as we bounce around.

One Final Request:

We love hearing from people. Please send us your stories, thoughts, comments, ideas, experiences, suggestions, and even complaints... although we hope there won't be many of those. Send them to KayandSteve@ConversationOnNetworking.com.

Give and you will get.

Personal Choice

Fun

Planning

Fun

Practice

Fun

Flexibility

And did we mention Fun?

Network away....................

CHAPTER 1 – USING THIS BOOK

You probably have noticed that this is a short chapter. That's because it's really easy to use this book. There are only a few things we wanted to mention. Well, Kay wanted to mention. Steve thought we should leave you to figure it out yourself.

FIRST:

Although we put the chapters in some sort of order, there really is no need to read this book from beginning to end. Each chapter largely stands on its own, so read in whatever order seems useful to you. If you come across a reference to something you haven't read yet, don't worry about it. You'll find it later. You can even use some chapters as preparation for specific events or as a tune up if you feel your skill is drooping.

SECOND:

Practice. If you want to improve your skills you need to practice.

Do it.
Often.

There is no excuse for saying "I'm just too busy," or "I never have any time." Ensuring that you develop and maintain great relationships to help you through life seems pretty important to us. Turn off the television and get out into the world. These are skills that you can use with every person you meet.

THIRD:

Enjoy yourself. This is supposed to be fun. Treat it that way. You'll be surprised how people respond when you come across as energetic, enthusiastic, interested, and fun. Especially as compared to lethargic, dull, boring, and depressing! Think about how just reading the previous two sentences makes you feel. Which you do you want to show to the world?

Tip of the Page

Exhibit humor regularly.

Keep smiling.

FOURTH:

Find your own style. **There is no right or wrong.** Take the information we present and play with it until it's comfortable for you. If you're not comfortable, everyone you meet knows it. Generating discomfort is hardly the way to develop and maintain great relationships. Whatever works for you is right, no matter what anyone tells you. Just remember that fact when you share your success strategies, since they won't work for everyone.

Finally, it really is personal. The Internet doesn't replace actually meeting and developing relationships with people. And it's not book learning. It's going out into the world; remember... the real world, not the World Wide Web. It's connecting with real people. You never know what might develop.

One more thing: some chapters are more concrete than others. It's just the way some things are. So remember, even in those chapters, find your own way to what works for you.

Steve's father Hal recently had to have some surgery. Hal is a gregarious fellow. He's a psychologist who spent his career in the business consulting world. I won't share how old he is, but it's been a few years since he retired after working well into his 70s. So there he is, laying on the gurney getting prepped for surgery. Of course he talks to the anesthesiologist. Next thing you know he's being invited to address the Anesthesiologist Association on using hypnosis for pain relief, especially as related to surgery. Unfortunately, they still charged him for the operation.

Tip of the Page

Networking is a verb!

(We figured we might as well start you off right):

Look at your calendar for the next month. Figure out where you're going to schedule some time each week to read this book and practice these skills. Schedule it.

Exercise #2:

Think about your behavioral style. Maybe you've completed a style assessment. If so, take it out and review it. Jot down a few things that make you comfortable and a few to avoid. As you read through this book, use this as a guide to modify our ideas in ways that will be most comfortable for you.

There is no right or wrong way.

Do whatever works for you.

CHAPTER 2 – WHAT'S NEW?

So there we were. In the middle of the driest place on earth, our little bus hanging off the cliffs. Me and a bunch of MBA students. And it was only ten more hours to go until we reached Cotahuasi, Peru, an oasis in the mountains at 14,000 feet.

It never ceases to amaze us how many people pass right by the greatest opening ever: **What's New?**

The hardest thing to do is to catch someone's attention, to cause him or her to stop and really listen. It seems that generally when you're asked, "How ya doin'?" "What's up?" "What's happening?" or the one you now know we like best, "What's new?" It's just a courtesy. The trick is to actually answer the question in a way that grabs them. My goal is to literally stop them in their tracks.

There's always something happening in your life. Something wonderful or something you need or something you'd like to share. Use this to give yourself a chance to create a strong connection... a positive connection. It seems that people find it easier to complain and share lousy experiences rather than great experiences. We don't know why. If there's anyone who can explain this, please let us know.

What we do know is that it's impossible to create a wonderful, positive, energizing connection with someone by sharing really depressing information. So think it through. Prepare. Always have a couple of interesting and uplifting or humorous stories to share about something recent that happened. It doesn't even have to have happened to you. Perhaps you heard something really interesting on the radio, or passed something new and different on the way to work. I happened to go past a restaurant on the edge of The University of Pennsylvania campus that only sells cereal! It's called, surprise, Cereality. It was a great topic for quite a while.

Tip of the Page

Only if you're dead is it okay to say "nothing" when asked, "What's new?"

Keep your first
words short and
enigmatic ...
get them to stop
and ask you for
more information.

Every morning think of something interesting you did, learned, or saw the day before and share it with someone before lunch.

It really doesn't matter what it is as long as it catches someone's attention. Now, having said that, you can be really clever about what you're sharing. No reason not to have it lead to something you want people to know, say a new service you provide or a new product you're selling, or that they're invited to a party next week. You can even make it something you need, but make it simple — use just a few words, "I'm looking for a great hotel in San Francisco" or "I need to rent a car in France, have you done that?"

You probably noticed that my little story about Peru sort of starts and stops in the middle of nowhere... just like the trip. I've gotten a lot of mileage out of it. First of all, it's short so I can get it all out while they're still listening. And then I've got them. I've yet to find anyone who doesn't ask me what I'm talking about. And once they ask a question, it's okay to continue.

As you probably realize by now, we're consultants. We're always looking for work and tooting our own horns... just a little. The rest of Steve's story (short version) goes like this:

What was I doing there? Oh, well, I'm now on the faculty of The Wharton School and I lead an MBA marketing seminar. I led my class to meet with some Peruvian students we were working with, and then we all went up into the high mountains to meet with some farmers who are descendents of the Incas. We completed a wonderful project to help them find markets in the United States for their organic products.

They've given me the okay to keep talking. They've even requested that I keep talking. With their consent, I've managed to share many wonderful things: I'm now part—a very minor part but what the heck— of a world famous business school, I know something about marketing, I know how to be a professor... well, sort of. What else did I manage to share?

everal things can happen next. They could say "interesting" in a bored way and that's that. For some reason not everyone finds me and my stories enthralling. Unfortunately, you'll probably find the same thing about you and your stories. Don't be discouraged. There are other people out there who will find you and your story exciting and stimulating.

Or they could continue to ask questions. We're developing a relationship and I'm imparting information about myself in a non-threatening, non-sales way. And every now and then someone says, "I'd really like to have lunch and talk with you more."

Practice:

Make a list of five things that are new and interesting. Think about whom you might share them with. Not people you already know, although that's okay, too, but in what places they would be appropriate. What can you share with the person who sits next to you at the Starbucks? What can you share with the waiter at lunch? What's a good plane conversation starter?

More practice:

If you're really organized, track what happens as you spout your little snippets of fun things. Which ones cause people to become interested? What gets things thrown at you? Work at it until it's natural to always have something interesting to say in response to whatever throwaway greeting you hear.

After all that work Steve owes it to you to finish his story so...

I'm pleased to report that we were very successful in finding out everything necessary to export agricultural products to the United States and meet organic standards. We even managed to set up meetings with a number of interested buyers. As a side benefit, we began to develop an opportunity for ecotourism. Visit Cotahuasi and have the experience of a lifetime.

Tip of the Page

Think about what you want to achieve...you probably should use a different response if you're looking for a date than if you're in the job market.

Life always brings you something new and interesting.

CHAPTER 3 = BE POSITIVE

We met someone the other day. To our great amazement he immediately shared this story with us: "Hi, I'm John. Nice to meet you both. I'm glad I got here since I've been very sick. First I had to have an emergency appendectomy. While they were doing the surgery they noticed a few other problems. I seem to have liver cancer too. So they did another operation. Then I started chemotherapy and radiation treatments. You might notice that all my hair has fallen out. I've been so stressed by this that I've had three auto accidents recently. I think my divorce is ready to be finalized. Too bad I don't have enough money to pay the attorneys, but I guess one more lawsuit against me won't be any big deal. So, enough about that, I hear you guys are great networkers and can set me up with some contacts."

Well, wasn't it fun to meet John? Feel your shoulders hunching? Does your stomach ache? Does your head hurt? And you don't even know John.

Before we go any further we need to help you out.

DO THIS NOW:

Stand up.

Walk a couple of steps.

Swing your arms and twist your body a little.

Take a few deep, deep breaths.

Feel better? Breathing deeply and moving around a little is great stress relief... especially from people who suck up all your energy. And you can even do this while they're talking to you.

Maybe John is a little extreme, but we've all met people who share such intimate and draining information with us as soon as they meet us. Just like John, they seem to be totally oblivious to the reaction this causes in the listener. Most people react just like you did... they look for the closest exit and run, not walk, to escape. Hopefully you've already learned the lesson but just in case you need some reinforcement...

People like happy people. They like to hear about good things and smile and laugh with you. If you make people happy they want to be around you. They probably don't even have a conscious idea of why this is; they just know that you're fun to be with. It doesn't take people long to decide if they like you, so remember that you only have that famous one chance to make a first impression... make it a good one.

It's a lot more fun to be with upbeat people.

Negative stories shove people away...

Positive stories bring them closer.

Exercise:

Every morning wipe away everything bothering you until you feel able to meet people smiling. You might even write these negative things on the mirror before you brush your hair and then really wipe them out.

You might already be tired of hearing this, but guess what... it's all about planning and practice. You want to become so full of good stories and things to say that there is no way for a negative story to ever approach your lips when you meet people. Now remember, we're talking about meeting people and developing strong ongoing relationships for business and life. It's perfectly okay to seek support and share problems with people like best friends and relatives. We even have people whose job it is to listen to you in difficult circumstances... we call them pastors or therapists.

So don't kill off potential relationships before they get going. Smile, laugh, share nice thoughts and experiences, and offer solutions to problems. Leave everyone you meet more energized than when you met them. Fill up their battery rather than run it down.

Practice Bad Energy Discharge:

Do the breathing exercise we mentioned earlier. Practice until you can discharge stress by merely wiggling your fingers so you can do it anywhere, anytime, anyplace.

If you're afraid to smile too much, see the dentist more often.

Notice that everything that happens to you has a good side. Sometimes it's not obvious, but it's there somewhere. Spend an entire day discovering the good in everything that happens to you.

Practice storytelling:

The next five times someone tells you something that sounds like the story that began this chapter, reframe it for them. Turn it into something that has a positive message and can uplift and energize whoever hears the story.

I recently decided I should sell my house. Now this is a very traumatic experience, since I live on a big property in the middle of the woods, on a dirt road, in horse country, in a house I've mostly built with my own two hands. I love where I live and the people I know. But circumstances sometimes dictate that we move on. For a while when I told people about this I think I was John. But now I've reframed the experience and it's actually become a lot of fun to talk to people about the next stage of my life and the new and exciting adventures awaiting me. I've figured out how to completely reverse the message... and it's a lot more energizing for me too.

INTERESTING LAST THOUGHT:

It takes less energy to smile than to frown.

CHAPTER 4 = TOO MANY PLACES TO GO, TOO LITTLE TIME

The other day, I met someone who rushed up to me. He was frantic. Now I get a lot of unusual questions and odd requests, but this was the first time I remembered being asked to save someone's marriage. And what was the problem? This poor fellow had heard that he needed to go to a breakfast event every morning and a meeting every evening if he wanted to meet people and be successful. His wife thought he was having an affair. He was so frazzled that he told me he never met anyone at these things but was determined to make it work for him... whatever that means.

We think this is nuts.

We give you permission to *not* attend things. Let me repeat this: We give you permission to *not* attend things. If your gut screams "No," listen. Your gut knows best. Really. We have yet to run into someone who tells us "my gut said no, I did it anyway, and my gut was wrong." On the other hand, there are uncountable stories that start "my gut said no, I did it anyway; boy was my gut right."

Okay, you decided to go in spite of all this. Why are you going? If you can't come up with a good answer, please don't go. You'll just be wasting your time. It doesn't have to be a spectacular answer, just a good answer. "Because there are going to be some people I like to talk to there" is fine. We like to go places just to talk to people too.

"Because I'm interested in working in this industry and have determined that there will be several people I need to meet in attendance" sounds like

---

Here are some reasons not to go. Feel free to add to this list.

10. The last twenty times you've gone to this meeting you've fallen asleep within the first ten minutes.

9. You already have an attorney, accountant, realtor...

8. You've never been to an industry meeting where you met a great prospect.

7. You can afford to buy your own bagel and coffee.

6. You've discovered that you can't form relationships with 86 new people in fourteen minutes of networking time.

5. You've already attended fourteen similar events this week... and so far met no interesting people.

4. You have over four thousand people already on your "I need to follow up" list.

3. If they're such experts why are they asking you to give them money instead of just buying real estate themselves?

2. You remember that every time you go to this event no one is having fun... including you.

1. You could use a good nap.

If you go to an event or meeting with someone, split up. It improves your chances of meeting someone interesting.

a pretty good reason. "Because I'm determined to expand the number of people I know and will come back with four great contacts to meet for lunch" seems good to me. Notice how the more specific you get, the more pressure you put on yourself and the more planning you need to do in advance.

It really doesn't matter what the reason is, as long as you know what it is and have thought about what outcome you'd like to achieve by the time the meeting is over, and going has at least as much value as what you'd do if you didn't go... see number one above.

The very first time we presented *Conversation On Networking* we received the most amazing e-mail testimonial. "I had an epiphany while at your show. You've given me back hours each week." We didn't have a clue what this person was talking about. So we found out. It seems that our epiphany experiencing person was someone like the fellow we met at the beginning of this chapter. After spending time listening to us — (we're always a useful meeting to attend, by the way) — he thought about this issue. He arrived home and immediately did what we had suggested, he thought about places he went and figured out what he got out of going to them. Sure enough, he discovered lots of wasted effort he could eliminate.

You only have so much time... use it wisely.

Practice:

Write down three good reasons for attending the next few meetings you're invited to or places you were thinking of going. If you can't come up with three good reasons, or maybe one great reason, seriously consider whether it's worth your time to go.

Comparative Practice:

After doing the above, make a second column and write down what you'd do if you didn't go. Which list is more compelling?

Daring Practice:

Skip a boring meeting and see what happens.

CHAPTER 5, PART A =
I'M REALLY SHY, BORING, QUIET...

So there I was. Leaving an association meeting where I had just spent an entire day with hundreds of people, all involved in my business. I'd had a good time. I'd attended several interesting and educational seminars, discovered the hotel made a great Caesar Salad for lunch, sampled some new and exciting wines at the cocktail hour, and heard a keynote speech after dinner that put me to sleep... but I needed a nap, since I'd be up all night doing the work I'd skipped by being at the meeting. And then it hit me. I hadn't met one new person. Everyone I'd talked to was either in passing — as in please pass the butter — or was someone I've known for years.

We're sure this has happened to some of you out there in reader land. Sometimes we call this the introvert issue. Those extroverts go to things, meet everyone, and come back with handfuls of business cards. Sometimes they actually even remember some of the people they met... and sometimes they even see these people again. But you're not like that. You like to sit back, watch what's going on, be approached rather than approach someone, and be with people you already know. The great skill you already have is developing wonderful long relationships, but first you need the initial introduction, right?

Let's talk about how to create more of these initial meetings in a comfortable way. We want you to start by reframing yourself: you're not shy, boring, or quiet. You're reserved, intriguing, and knowledgeable. And since you're actually such an interesting person, you owe it to others to let them see how wonderful and useful it will be to get to know you. Stop selfishly hiding yourself away.

Tip of the Page

Eveyone you know now you once met for the first time.

Exercise:

Try this new concept of yourself on for size. Talk to yourself about it. Practice being intriguing. Begin with your dog and move on to strangers. Remember to take note of how you feel and the difference in the way other people treat you.

It's amazing
how the more
prepared you are
the easier it is.

Most people are uncomfortable meeting people, even many extroverts. Really. It's a difficult thing to do. So to do it well you need to be prepared. Elsewhere in this book we talk about ways to prepare, such as creating a few introductions for your own self. You could look there now or find it later. Your choice. Just like you really do have the choice about how to think of yourself.

Even extremely experienced actors and salespeople get butterflies in their stomach. Many people think of this as a sign of nervousness. It's not. It's your body getting ready to participate in a new and exciting experience; skydiving, ballroom dancing, or meeting new people. When you think of it this way, it becomes exhilarating rather than debilitating.

At a show we did, Sarah told us this story.

> "I'm an engineer. I've been working a long time and am quite experienced and expert in my specialty. I decided to go to the annual meeting of my association. Everything was going along fine until the night of the Gala. I opened the door to the ballroom, looked in, saw five hundred guys in blue suits, turned around, went up to my room, and sat on the bed. There was no way I was going in there.
> But then I remembered. I'd paid a lot of money to come to this event and I decided I was going to get my money's worth. I thought about it and realized that everyone at the Gala was an engineer. There were probably lots of guys just as nervous as I was. It occurred to me that they would do just what I would do and feel just like I felt, overwhelmed and uncomfortable. They were probably down there right now doing what I felt like doing, standing around the walls by themselves. So I decided to go back, walk around the perimeter, and introduce myself to everyone standing by themselves. And I had a marvelous time."

Practice:

Think about the last event or events you went to. What could you have done in advance to better prepare yourself to meet people? Use this knowledge to prepare yourself for the next few things you attend.

Variation on above practice:

Think about the last few times you met, or had the opportunity to meet but couldn't bring yourself to meet, someone. How could you have been better prepared for a random meeting? Use this knowledge to prepare yourself for any opportunity you might have to meet someone.

Daring Exercise:

Go to a meeting that you have never gone to before. Introduce yourself to many people and see what happens.

> We all have a fantastically interesting person inside.

The person you're *not* introducing yourself to is probably just as uncomfortable as you are. Help them out.

CHAPTER 5, PART B = I CAN'T SHUT UP

So there I was. Watching this guy run around to people sharing his story. As near as I can tell he never once let anyone share their story with him. He even followed people, speaking to their back as they tried to escape. He was determined to finish his story since he was clearly convinced it was a wonderful story that everyone needed and wanted to hear. No way was anyone going to escape.

Ever meet this guy? Of course you have. Did you think we were going to let the extroverts off without making them sit down, be quiet, and listen to some advice?

Extroverts have an interesting problem... they're in the minority. You might not believe it since they take up so much airtime, but most people, the vast majority of people, are not extroverts. Extroverts have great difficulty understanding what this means so they just extrovert over everyone.

So this chapter is the flip side of *"I'm Really Shy, Boring, and Quiet."* Now I know that all of you outgoing folk are already tired of reading this, but persevere. The most important skill you need to learn is patience. Slow down. It takes time for most people to get to know you, process information, and decide what to do next. If you want to establish strong and long lasting relationships, you need to be able to modify your behavior to meet the needs of whomever you're talking to.

Tip of the Page

When your mouth is working your ears aren't.

Exercise:

Go to an event and don't talk to anyone at all. Then do it again, but this time, only ask people questions. Think about how different this is than the way you usually feel at events.

It's hard to slow down and listen. It's also hard to learn anything when you're talking. Relationships develop from mutual interests. How can you find out what these are without asking questions and listening?

Introverts know the value of quiet time. It's the opportunity for your brain to relax and process information. This takes as long as it takes. They also know that sometimes speaking slowly and taking your time in explaining things is a great way to deliver information.

For a whole week, don't interrupt anyone for any reason... unless their coat is on fire.

Rush, rush, rush. There's never enough time. That's why there are lots of people that need a follow-up... a note, a call, or worse yet, a lunch. Lots of random contacts are not as useful as fewer contacts who really know you. How can someone know enough to refer you or introduce you or even remember you if they've only met you once? And they probably tuned out half, or more, of what you said if you're the person at the beginning of this chapter.

You undoubtedly have a great collection of skills and tremendous knowledge about something. What's the most effective way to let people you meet know about this?

Exercise:

Figure out three things that you want people to know about you and write them down. Yes, write them down. These are the only things you can tell the next few people you meet and you have to do it with one sentence for each thing. Keep the sentences short. Then you have to be quiet until they tell you three things about themselves. However long it takes them.

Notice that so far I've been using short paragraphs and sentences in this chapter. I'm writing for you folks, and you know who you are. This chapter is aimed at short attention spans. Short attention spans.

Isn't it interesting that the people who talk the longest have the shortest attention spans? They ramble around until something clicks. Anything. So it's hard for others to figure out what they really do and why to develop a relationship with them.

Tip of the Page

Networking is not a timed sport... or a contact sport.

If there's time to
meet new people,
why isn't there
time to connect
with those you
already know?

Talking *at* people is like hitting them over the head until they agree... and then wondering why they don't follow through. It is not networking.

Practice Makes Perfect:

Figure out three things that you want people to know about you and write them down. Yes, write them down. These are the only things you can tell the next few people you meet and you have to do it with one sentence for each thing. Short sentences. Then you have to be quiet until they tell you three things about themselves. However long it takes them.

Some of you might notice we already did the above practice. It's repeated because I know that you skipped over it the first time. You really do have to think about and practice these things if you want to improve your ability to develop relationships with most of the people you meet.

I suggest you do this exercise again too:

For one week, don't interrupt anyone for any reason...unless a train is about to run them down... and I don't mean you.

Listen. Did I already mention listening? Were you paying attention? You can't learn anything from anybody unless you listen.

Another Exercise:

For the next few people you meet, wait until the next day and then jot down a few things they told you. Is there a blank page staring back at you?

Okay, enough of this. You get the picture. Since this is a short chapter to go with short sentences and paragraphs, feel free to read it again.

Silence is
Golden

CHAPTER 6 – THE ART OF MEETING LOGISTICS

I went to a meeting the other day. Actually it was more of a big summer business party. This morning I got a call from someone I met there. I was excited until I realized he was telling me that he's beaten the stock market by an average of 10 percent a year for the last five years. Yup, the financial advisor sales routine. If this is the only person I met that leads to a call, unless I'm looking for a financial advisor – which I'm not – I just failed my own test of a successful meeting: one where I meet at least one person I'd like to see again.

It is possible to successfully navigate a meeting of any kind. It is possible to have a great time, meet people you'd like to keep it touch with, and accomplish some business or personal objectives. Of course, this means you need to spend some time on preparation and planning (here they are again). And the first thing you need to do is figure our why you're going. (See *Chapter Four – "Too Many Places To Go, Too Little Time."*) This might sound simplistic, but we can't tell you how many times we're told the reason someone goes to a meeting is because they've always gone, or they heard you're supposed to go, or someone told them to be successful you need to attend at least 12 events a week. So far no winning answers.

Even after reading this and the chapter *"Too Many Places To Go, Too Little Time,"* you've decided to go. Okay. It happens.

If we think about this like we're planning a military maneuver, what's the first step? Reconnoiter the terrain. Figure out who's there. From a networking standpoint, the most important task of effectively attending a meeting is to find out who is going to be there that you want to meet. So go early. Scout out the table with the nametags. Or even better, contact the organizer in advance and see if you can get an attendee list. This is especially important if it's a big convention or meeting. You can only talk to so many people, so make sure they're the ones most important to achieving your outcome.

Tip of the Page

Treat everyone with respect; they might sit you with the speaker.

Go early and study the nametags on the registration table.

Generally you can go up to people and introduce yourself. Of course, if you can find someone to introduce you with some kind words, that's even better. Remember, you don't need to meet everyone. What's important is that you make two or three good connections... or even one good connection if it's the right one.

Always make friends with the person handing out the nametags and running the event. Let them know how great it is that they've done all this work and how excited you are to get the chance to talk to the people you've been trying to meet. You never know, maybe you'll wind up getting invited to sit at the head table.

So you're ready to enter the meeting room. It's a big place. Remember, you want to meet some specific people. Go to them first. Otherwise it's too easy to get stuck talking to people who you really don't want to spend time with.

If it's an organized meeting, plan where to sit. On the center aisle so you can catch everybody or in the back corner so you can watch everybody... and leave easily and unobtrusively if it's boring. Up front so the speakers will see you clearly, or near the rear so you blend in. Next to someone you want to meet, so there's no chance of them getting away. In an empty row and hope someone interesting sits next to you. It all makes a difference in the result you'll get from attending the meeting. Think it through in advance.

Practice:

For the next few meetings you attend alternate being the first person to arrive at a meeting with arriving exactly on time... no, I won't suggest arriving late. Think about the different experiences you have.

Plan:

Actually write a few ideas down for why you are attending the meeting and what you expect to get out of attending. Do this for three or four meetings and then go to a meeting without doing it. Which result do you like better?

Practice:

Figure out where to be to ensure you meet the speakers you want to meet. Prepare a question or comment for each speaker so you actually get their attention when you introduce yourself. Of course, you can do this last piece anytime there are speakers.

I went to an event not so long ago. Coming early, of course, I was standing in front of a naked nametag table. Suddenly this woman appeared, looking harried and carrying a box full of nametags. She told me how sorry she was that everything was running late and would I give her a minute to get organized. So I pitched in and helped her arrange the nametags. While we did this I asked her about the speaker, who was someone I wanted to meet. She told me she would introduce me. Not only that, she said there was an extra seat at the head table and would I be interested in sitting with the speaker.

A big meeting just means a bigger waste of time if you're not prepared.

Where you sit changes what you get...
and if you can sneak out unobtrusively.

CHAPTER 7 – IT'S BEEN FOREVER

The trouble with watching the pot is that it takes forever to boil. Or so they say. Interestingly enough, these same folk tell us that if you slip a lobster into the pot, it will boil before it realizes what happened. As odd as it might seem, both of these ideas are also true when we're talking about developing and deepening great relationships... for business or life.

Tip of the Page

Process means something is happening... you must apply energy.

Test:

Boil a pot of water. We won't include a recipe since we never really believe those people who say they can't even boil water. This exercise actually has two parts:

1. Boil water while doing something else.
2. Do it again while watching the pot the entire time.

Notice which seems to take longer...
and which results in better boiled water.

You can't rush a relationship, although you can help it along. Good things take as long as they take. So your job is to manage the process along the best path as it wanders through e-mail, lunch, cards, calls, another lunch... or maybe breakfast, until it happens: the opportunity for a job, a sale, or maybe a date. What you need to do is figure out how to balance what happens in the pot... keep it heating without watching so closely that you become bored, while making sure that you don't wind up cooked because you just weren't paying enough attention.

It's an ongoing process. This means you need to become flexible and learn to balance many relationships at all different stages of development. This is as much science as art.

Neighbors are
people too:
do you know
what they do?

The art is continuing to be clever and interesting so the object of your attention wants to keep talking to you. The science is to track it all so you don't either go crazy or lose track of what's going on or both. Somewhere in this book there's a chapter or two on the science part. That seems to mean this chapter must be about the art side so...

Art is a wonderful thing. No two people look at the same painting, sculpture, or play and see exactly the same thing. We take our experience and add it in to create something unique to our view. So the art of relationships and networking means that no two people will ever do it exactly the same way. That's fine. Your goal is to figure out what works best for you. So start by figuring out what you hope to achieve from networking.

Exercise:

Make a list. Right now before you read any further. What is it you want from your own personal art of networking?

Okay. So now you have a list. It's a good place to start, but remember that networking is often a random process. Don't get all carried away with structure here, we're in the art chapter. Look at your list. Are these outcomes that are comfortable for you? Are they related to relationships? This is an important question since we want to get rid of the transactions, at least for purposes of networking. Networking is a process. This means it goes on and on and on and on. It weaves outward, tying in more and more strands as time goes by.

Transactions stop the process. They are one-time events. They can be wonderful, enlightening, fun, and rewarding, but they're probably not networking. We say probably because you never know, but generally a transaction is not going to lead to an ongoing relationship, although it may be part of an ongoing relationship. Notice: transactions within a relationship are one thing; transactions instead of a relationship are quite another thing.

Be patient.

Good things develop over time.

Being helpful fuels networking.

Helping others is a great way to keep a process going. Most folk are happy to hear from people who have helped them in some way. This can even be a way to turn a transaction into a process.

Be prepared for it to take awhile. Be prepared to end a relationship if it runs out of gas. Just because it's a relationship doesn't mean it's worthwhile to continue. Everyone falls in and out of connection with people during the networking process. We would like you to know it's happening and work at making sure the good ones continue and that you end the bad ones.

It's a marathon, not a sprint.

Practice:

Make a list of people you know. Not just relatives or co-workers, but people from all aspects of your life. Figure out where you are in the ongoing relationship with them. Are they a good source of referrals? Is it time to take them to lunch? Do you even know why you stay in touch with some of them?

Project:

Develop a plan to deepen relationships with some folk who can help you in work or other situations. Try it out and see what happens.

CHAPTER 8 =
THERE IS A BENEFIT TO LISTENING

I'M having a great time. Here I am on a nice evening, wandering around at an outdoor technology association party celebrating the beginning of summer. There must be five hundred people, a collection of executives from technology companies, as well as their major vendors. A band is playing, drinks are flowing, and people are networking like crazy. Over on one side a co-sponsor has a table set up with some information, so I wander over to see what they do. Big mistake.

I introduce myself to the two people working the table. They're talking to each other since there is no one else there. I soon find out why they're alone. I mention that I'm not a technology person so would like a one minute, non-technological overview of what they do. The man seems to be the boss and launches into one general sentence that I follow, understand, and fully answers my request. Without pause he then immediately launches into rapid fire, unstoppable technical descriptions so dense that I don't think he's even speaking English anymore.

I attempt to stop him. I interrupt and tell him that he's not listening to me. I have all I need. He ignores me and continues his harangue. I appeal to his assistant. She rolls her eyes and shrugs. I persevere in my quest to shut him up. It becomes a challenge. After all, I'm supposed to be an expert at this and I'm overwhelmed. His assistant is now openly laughing. Finally he needs to breathe and I give him a short lecture on listening to his audience. He clearly doesn't hear a thing I've said, since he again begins to spew technical details at me as I wander away shaking my head. What's particularly bizarre is that I actually understand what they do and think they really do have a unique way of helping their clients. But will I refer them? I never took a card and can't remember their names or even the company name. But he sure did make an impression on me.

Tip of the Page

Strong relationships are a two way street.

Learn to
appreciate silence
in a conversation.
You can often see
people thinking,
but you rarely
can hear their
brain working.

More and more people seem to think that the appropriate way to connect with someone is the cable news method... jump up and down, wave your arms, and scream loudest. Wear them down rather than connect with them and use facts and ideas and emotion to make your point. And forget about actually asking a question or attempting to find out what their interests are and how you can help solve their problems. This sure isn't networking. Networking is a process of developing a relationship that flows both ways. Each side has something to offer the other. It's mutually beneficial. If it's not, it won't develop into a lasting relationship. The best way to ensure that you connect with someone is to help them out. The most important skill isn't talking, it's listening. And not just listening, but hearing and understanding what you hear... not only the words but also the feelings and nuances behind the words.

In my story, it was all about him rather than me. He's learned one way to introduce himself, his company, and his products... high speed, high volume, and high detail. There's no place for questions or for understanding the person he's talking at. Reminds me of all those used car salesmen stories.

Maybe the hard sell works for certain kinds of products, but I guarantee you that selling yourself and trying to establish an ongoing relationship isn't one of them. Take it easy, learn to calibrate what's going on in the conversation, and notice the effect you're having on the other person. Remember that it's about them, not you.

Exercise:

Go to a nice restaurant by yourself at lunchtime, sit in a corner facing the entire restaurant, and watch the different tables. Try and figure out which groups are sales lunches, which are old friends catching up, and who's in charge at each table. Track the dynamic as it ebbs and flows. Who's having fun and who looks like they're being beaten up?

We've noticed that most people seem to find talking about themselves to be the most interesting topic imaginable. Take advantage of this. It's much easier to establish a good relationship by asking questions and listening intently to their answers, than by spewing mountains of odd facts about yourself. Be interested, genuinely interested. Who knows, you might even learn something.

Most people operate at a moderate pace, or even slower than moderate. They need time to think and integrate information. Help them out. Watch how fast you're talking. Allow silence to linger. It's okay to have quiet space in a conversation. But stay engaged. Don't look around as though you're bored. If you are, why are you trying to engage this person? Move on and save both of you time and energy.

Tip of the Page

There's a reason you have two ears and only one mouth.

Establishing relationships isn't selling. It's connecting on an emotional level. It's up to you to figure out how to modify your style so you can be successful with many different people. Everyone is different... different interests, different needs, different likes, and different dislikes. Sure, we all share some things, but in each of us it's packaged differently.

Differences in each of us mean we each require our own message. Successful networkers know how to be flexible and modify themselves and their message to accommodate the different requirements of each person they meet. They learn many ways to approach people and become expert at watching and listening. Notice the response you get. If it isn't what you'd like to see, it's your problem, not the problem of the other person.

Practice:

As you meet people alternate telling them your story and asking them to tell you theirs. Vary the pattern. Try talking first and listening second. Try it the other way. Try not telling your story at all, but just getting them to talk.

Tip
of the
Page

The person
most interested
in hearing your
voice is you
(*and maybe
your Mother*).

More practice:

Watch people talking from across a room. Try and judge what they're thinking, at least the big ideas. Are they interested in the conversation, bored, having fun? Is the subject intense or light? If it's a place where you think its ok, go and ask them and see if you were right.

Extra Credit Practice:

Try and ensure that the next five people you meet leave laughing. Note: If you're going to practice connecting on an emotional level, always, always, always work on positive, pleasant, humorous outcomes. Not only is it what you want to achieve, but you'll live longer.

I was going to buy a new car a couple of years ago. Notice that I was *going* to buy a new car, not just *thinking* about it. Talk about a great prospect. I have a few friends with Subarus™ and figured I'd go to the local dealer. Figuring all new cars are pretty good mechanically these days, I decided if I found one in the right color with a great cup holder, I'd buy it.

I walk into the dealer and talked to the first salesman who approaches me. I tell him what I'm looking for and we walk over to a floor model. He tries to show me the engine because they apparently have a wonderful engine. I tell him several times that I don't care and just want to see the cup holder since they have the bright red color I want in the model that seems right. He continues to insist that I look at the engine, so I tell him I'm leaving and walk out.

I find myself caught by the manager as I attempt to leave. He asks me why I'm leaving. I tell him that the salesman keeps insisting that I look at the engine and I don't care about that. He tells me "I make sure everyone looks at the engine because it's so cool. Come on back and I'll show you." I look at him with amazement, leave, and drive over to another dealer with cars I've admired.

Next time you see me, ask me to show you my bright red SAAB with the great cup holder. I'll take you for a ride but promise I won't try and get you to look under the hood, because I don't even know how to open it without getting out the manual.

Tip of the Page

Calibrate your audience... you'll see when you're connecting.

CHAPTER 9 –
YOU MUST BE KIDDING

Sometimes we do wonder if people have been listening... or if they've spent the last hour or two in an alternate universe only they can see. As you know if you've been paying attention while reading this book, or have had the exceptional good fortune to see us in real life, we spend a lot of time talking about developing relationships over time. The idea of networking as relationship building lies at the heart of everything we do and talk about. So you can imagine our surprise when...

Tip of the Page

Any interruption breaks the flow. Good if you're talking to a jerk, not so good if it's a prospective customer or date.

We were reaching the end of a show. It was a little unusual since it was a public event and there were a large number of job seekers, or People in Transition, in the audience. It kept us on our toes since quite a few of the questions were tinged with a little bit of desperation. There were a lot of questions that verged on requests for therapy. But with our good nature and humor we managed to answer everything and help people with our usual wonderful advice. And then it happened. Someone, not a Person in Transition I might add, wanted to know how long they had to wait upon first meeting someone to ask for work for their company. They thought five minutes is sufficient. Of course, they also let us know that it wasn't a very successful strategy. Did we have any advice?

Did we have any advice? We always have advice. We'd been giving out advice on just this very topic for the last hour. So we reiterated some of it and then moved along. But it got us thinking: **Paying attention.**

We really hadn't discussed paying attention with people. Since Steve is one of those people who needs computer directions to start with "turn on the computer," we couldn't believe we'd missed such an elementary step.

So, you're reading this because you want to improve your skill at networking with people, developing great relationships that can lead to something wonderful... in business or life. How can you ever expect this to happen if you're not paying attention? Forget multi-tasking. Multi-tasking means doing all the things you're doing simultaneously equally poorly. That's equally poorly, not equally well.

You need to show people you are interested in them, that you are focused on them. For the moment, at least, they are the center of your universe. This means: turn off your cell phone or set it on vibrate... but don't look at it while talking to them. Don't send messages on your Blackberry, don't look at your pager. Focus on the person you're talking to. They will remember that you treated them this way. It's called respect. Or maybe even what we used to call good manners.

You develop strong and lasting relationships by showing respect for other people. They are important to you. Let them know this by how you act in their presence, by how you treat them. We think the rudest thing you can do is answer your phone while talking to someone you're supposedly networking with. And mostly people do this without even offering an apology. Someone made the effort to actually show up and talk to you. And you're having them watch while you talk to someone clearly more important. The person on the phone is just lobbing in a call without any consideration to what the recipient is doing. That's why the most wonderful invention of recent times is... voice mail, if not the off button.

If there really is an emergency call you're waiting for, let them know. Apologize in advance that you're waiting to hear when to rush off to the hospital to meet your wife at the delivery room. You've not only told them that you respect the time they will spend with you and apologize for any interruptions, you've had an opportunity to introduce a little human interest into the relationship. It's a story that you both will always share... especially if you actually do get that call while meeting with them.

If you pay attention, you'll probably learn more.

If you can't pay attention, why are you there?

Be Totally
There,
Wherever
You Are

*J*ust so you don't think we forgot where we started this chapter, remember that developing relationships is a process. It means paying attention over time. Trying to rush the process is more likely to end it than to move it forward. Unfortunately, each relationship develops at it's own pace. It's not a highway, it's a winding path that often has loops and pauses and even some backtracks. Sometimes a great lead happens immediately, but sometime it takes years. As we say elsewhere, this should be fun. If it's a fun relationship there's an ongoing reward — a good time — anything else is a bonus.

Practice:

Make an effort to watch what happens to people you're talking with in person when you answer your cell phone. Notice what they do, how they act, what they say. How does it change the dynamic?

Second Level Practice:

Do the above practice varying whether you warn whoever you're talking with in advance or apologize before answering the cell phone versus just suddenly ignoring them and answering the phone.

Focus Practice:

Totally focus on the person you are talking to. Do not let your eyes wander around the room. Do not stare at the TV in the corner of the restaurant. Try and get the other person to sit in the worst seat in the room… that is, you are in the corner facing out and they are facing you and the corner. They can't look at anything else but you. Or try it the other way. Notice in which seat you remember more of the conversation and if it's easier to establish or strengthen the relationship.

Chapter 10 =
Everyone's Important...
and Knows Someone

Even your
relatives know
other people.

Kay often meets people at the University and Whist Club in Wilmington, Delaware. It's a wonderful old place with a nice dining room, bar, and some meeting rooms. They take good care of you while at the same time leaving you alone. Quite a balancing act and they do it well. One day, we met there for lunch. After lunch we decided we would enjoy sitting on the sun porch to do some business planning. At the end of a very productive meeting (places like this just seem conducive to great thinking), we decided to have a glass of wine before going off to evening events. There we sat as the club transitioned into the fine dining club they become in the evening. The dinner wait staff was sitting around the bar being treated to tastes of the evening's gourmet specials and the corresponding wines were being presented. Kay introduced Steve to the chef, as well as some of the other staff. The club manager immediately offered us the same wines that were being sampled, some of it well beyond our wine budget. A real treat, just for stopping and introducing nice people to each other.

You never know who is going to help you out.

So often, it's the least likely seeming person who helps you the most. It never ceases to amaze us how many people ignore or are even rude or nasty to receptionists, waiters and waitresses, executive assistants, bank tellers and the folk who work for airlines. Of course, this list goes on and on. Probably some of you work in a job that could be on this list. We commiserate with you. As a matter of fact, please send us your favorite story about how you dealt with the rude or nasty customer and maybe we'll use it in a future book... and send you a free copy, of course. Send it to KayandSteve @ConversationonNetworking.com. Thanks very much, in advance.

The most effective networkers know that you should always be polite to everyone you meet. Ask people their name, and remember it. Or, if like Steve, your memory doesn't always want to work well, write it down as part of your notes. And if that doesn't work, it's okay to be pleasant even if you don't remember their name. Of course, you can always **ask them to remind you** of their name.

Talk to them. Get to know them... just a little. Since most people do a good job of ignoring the so-called "little people" it will make an impression and they will have a nice memory of you. Even if it's someone you'll never see again, like the person at the airline check in counter, be nice. Of course, we don't expect you to remember the name of people you only meet once. As with everything else we say, use some common sense and figure out how our ideas work best for you.

In the old days, that is, before such good frequent flyer computer programs, Steve always used to get upgraded to first class, and even with today's computer systems that are always trying to keep him out of first class, he still manages it sometimes. His favorite time to approach the counter is after someone has been really nasty to the airline employee. It's positively breathtaking to see what happens when the first thing you say is "what a jerk that guy is." You've instantly created a bond with a harried person who probably had nothing to do with whatever the problem was. And it works everywhere.

Exercise:

Watch for opportunities to talk to a clerk just after they've been yelled at by a nasty customer. Commiserate and see what happens. (Unfortunately, these days you'll find lots of opportunities to practice this exercise. Think of your effort as bringing the world back into balance.)

The nice thing about being interested in everyone and friendly to all is that sometimes you make an instant connection, and get a first class upgrade or a free glass of wine. While these things are nice little immediate benefits, it's the long-term relationship that counts. If people feel so connected to you that they want to give you something, they'll remember you and help out in the future. Can't get through that gatekeeper to speak with the CEO? When was the last time you called the gatekeeper by name and just chatted?

People remember you and help you out because they like you. If it's their job, they'll do things for anyone, but not in the same way or with the same interest. And they surely won't make that extra effort we've just been discussing.

Everyone knows someone. This might sound obvious, but it's another one of those things that's right in front of you, but most people never think about it. People talk to other people, people are friends with other people, and people are even related to other people. And you don't have any idea who these other people are when you first meet someone.

So you need to be respectful to everyone because they might be the child of your boss. Or you might have an experience similar to what happened to Steve. He was sitting in the lobby of the Keo Plaza hotel in Tokyo minding his own business when another American started to chat with him. It quickly became clear to Steve that this was not someone he normally would want to spend any time with, but what the heck, it was Americans communing with each other in Japan. At some point in the conversation it happened. Steve realized that this person worked for someone he knew and was hoping to turn into a client. A little courtesy led to a useful connection. Bonding in a hotel lobby in Tokyo is a great way to establish a relationship. In case you're interested, this did eventually help lead to a new client.

We're all connected somehow.

Tip of the Page

Talk to everyone... afterward, you can decide who to avoid forever.

Bonus Tip of the Page

Spend time in fancy hotel lobbys – especially in exotic foreign cities.

Tip of the Page

Practice niceness. Never say anything nasty about anyone... you're probably talking to their best friend.

General Practice:

Spend a minute or two talking to everyone you meet. Ask them their name, something relevant to where you met them, or compliment them on something. Do whatever seems appropriate for the circumstances. Notice the change in them as you do this.

Business Practice:

Make it a point to talk to every receptionist, administrative assistant, mail room clerk you meet. Introduce yourself and ask them something about the company or their job or the city... even if it's where you both live. Do this either in person or when you call. One of the disadvantages of e-mail is that it's become much harder to do this; on the other hand, when you get the chance to do this you become even more memorable.

CHAPTER 11 – DO I HAVE TO?

Tip of the Page

If your gut says no, so should your mouth.

As you've noticed already, Steve used to go to Asia a lot, especially Japan. (He'd really like an excuse to go again, so keep him in mind if you want to establish a business there.) The Japanese are generally very polite people. They have a form and a ritual for everything. One of the more interesting things about Japan is the great difficulty they have in saying no. Not "no" in the sense of "I don't have any tuna sushi today," but no in the sense of "No, I won't buy anything from you so go away and leave me alone." Many people have commented on this. It has led to numerous business people making lots of costly trips to buy many Japanese executives expensive dinners in the hopes of making a sale. The reason being, the American couldn't read the Japanese cultural "no."

People in the United States say they're not like that. They know how to say no. They're impatient and don't have time to play these games. You probably say that about yourself. If it's actually true about you, we think you're in the minority of Americans. We don't have any statistics or research to back us up, just personal observation and the questions we get asked. And lots of people ask us how to say no.

It is very uncomfortable for people to say no. It's such an absolute rejection. People put themselves in the shoes of the person receiving the no and feel terrible. So instead of being straightforward and honest right up front, they hedge or even say okay. That is a big mistake. If it isn't going to work, it's better for everyone if they know it and can get on with their life.

As an example, do you agree to meet or at least talk every time you get a request for a networking meeting? If so, you must spend a lot of time talking to investment advisors, insurance agents, mortgage brokers, people in transition... It's okay to say no unless there's a mutual interest... you also need to feel you'll also get something out of the meeting. Now remember, just having a nice conversation is okay, as long as you know that's why you're agreeing to talk. And remember, you *do* need one investment advisor, insurance agent, mortgage broker...

The Value Proposition:

What value will you receive from a meeting or phone call?

IN the business world we often talk about The Value Proposition. It seems appropriate here. Although The Value Proposition sounds very impressive, for our purposes it's very simple: what value will you receive from – in this case – a meeting or phone call? Think about The Value Proposition every time an opportunity appears where you can meet someone new or further develop an existing relationship.

The other side of this decision to meet or not meet is what the meeting replaces. Would you do anything more interesting/useful/necessary/enjoyable if you didn't accept the invitation? Or would you just watch television? I find doing nothing is much better than accepting some invitations I receive.

Exercise:

Figure out The Value Proposition for the next ten people you meet. First decide if you'd like to meet them again. Then decide: What's in it for them? What's in it for you? Which of you is pushing the relationship and why? Compare this to your initial opinion of the relationship.

All interactions with people carry some risk. Some of the risk is opportunity cost, what you could be doing instead of being bored with this person. Some is the risk of sharing things that upon reflection you wish you'd kept secret. There's always the risk of trying to explain to your boss why lunch took three hours. Of course, there's also the possibility of a reward for meeting people. The reward of a sale. The reward of a wonderful lunch. The reward of just having some fun. The reward of making a new friend.

Exercise:

Figure out the Risk/Reward opportunity for the next ten meeting opportunities you face. Go to those where the reward is great; avoid those that seem to be all risk. Look back and evaluate the results of this exercise.

We all get asked for referrals. It goes with knowing people. We mention this after talking about Risk/Reward since this is a big issue with referrals. Often after a show someone comes up to us, tells us what they do in thirty seconds, and asks if we would refer them.

FIRST OF ALL:

They weren't paying attention (somewhere in this book we talk about the importance of paying attention) when we discussed referrals. How can anyone refer someone they just met?

SECOND:

How can I have any idea of what the person does, the quality of their work, their reliability, their pricing structure, and how they behave with clients? We would never put our own reputations on the line for someone we don't know well enough to be able to answer these questions... or at least have a pretty good idea of the answers.

Referrals come over time through strong relationships. It's important to ask people you know well for referrals so they remember to offer them, but you're asking people who can provide a real referral, who can describe you and what you do in enough detail to be credible and make you sound credible.

We get asked for references all the time when someone wants to hire us to present *Conversation On Networking, The Show.* References and referrals are similar... someone who knows you and is willing to tell that to other people. We always send names of people who have attended a show and/or hired us to do *The Show* in the past. It's the same thing. They can speak with authority and answer a few basic questions... in this case it's easy, all they have to do is mention how wonderful we are. Our references are always people who have real experience with what we do.

What's in it
for you is
an okay
question to ask.

Feeling good
is an okay answer.

IF it doesn't feel right, don't do it. Your gut is always right. It's okay to tell people that you aren't comfortable referring them since you don't really know what they can do. It's okay to tell someone you really don't have the time to meet with them. If they show you why it makes sense, you can always change your mind.

Practice:

The next few times you get asked to meet people, even if you know them well, ask why they want to meet with you. If you don't like the answer, keep drilling deeper until you either get an answer you like or decide to say no. Track how much time you save by not accepting all invitations to meet. Enjoy the naptime you collect his way.

Referral Practice:

We discussed above how to get out of giving referrals. Let's turn it around. Think about the people you know and decide on several who you can ask for referrals. It doesn't have to be earth shattering. If you're a corporate person ask for potential new business referrals (you don't have to be in sales to do this... it's amazing how differently management thinks of you if you're in the mailroom and start to bring in new business). Or ask for referrals to barbers or shoe stores. Listen carefully to the response you get and decide if it's a real referral or they're just afraid to say no.

CHAPTER 12 – FIRST MEETING

There we were, walking down Fifth Avenue in New York City at lunchtime on a nice spring day. There were hundreds, no... thousands, maybe even millions of people coming towards us from all directions. All those people shared a single trait. We didn't know any of them.

What an opportunity. Undoubtedly there were some really interesting people surrounding us. Musicians, actors, bartenders, manicurists, financial executives, college students, firefighters, taxi drivers, business owners, and who knows who else.

The world is full of people you've never met. Most of us started out life not knowing anyone... well, other than our mothers. With the exception of those of us living as hermits in the woods — who probably aren't reading this book anyway — we've all managed to meet lots of people along the way. Some have become good relationships and some not so good; some have lasted years or decades, while others barely lasted a few minutes.

All these meetings shared one thing: they happened. Somehow we each managed to figure out how to begin a conversation and then decide whether to continue it or not. But what opportunities passed us by because we weren't prepared to capture them?

Be Prepared.

The Boy Scouts say this. It's a great message for all of us. Mostly we've met people and established relationships randomly. By being prepared we can direct the process. Being prepared means that you've thought about who you are and what's important to you. You've thought about how you want to present yourself and what kinds of people you want to meet.

If you don't ask
you don't get.
That means
referrals as well as
most other things.

Think about what's important to you.
Write it down.
Think about how you want to present yourself.
Write it down.
Use this information to help you decide
who the people are with whom you want to develop
strong relationships.

And then there's practice. Preparation without practice gets you nowhere. Most of us aren't exceptional speakers able to automatically, on a moment's notice, speak authoritatively and convincingly to people we've just met about an important topic... ourselves. Those people, like politicians, known for this ability have writers and speech coaches and aides and have spent hours honing their message and learning their lines.

For some reason regular people think there's something wrong with preparation and practice. It reminds us of golfers. Amateurs always mention how lousy they are and then brag how they've never had a lesson and never practice while speaking in reverential tones about the pros that are so good. They always seem to miss the fact that the pros are good because they have coaches and practice all the time.

**Someone once told us
that the more they prepared
and practiced the luckier they got.

And so it is for meeting people.**

Be prepared for different situations.

You never know whom you'll meet or whom they know, so you have to be ready at all times, even for when you randomly meet someone on the street or in line. It's like our 'What's New' chapter. Never let an opportunity pass you by without having given yourself a great chance to connect.

Random meetings:

Always have a few interesting things that are important to you in mind to mention to people.

Planned events:

Think about why you are going and what you hope to accomplish. Think about the people that will be there. Create a couple of great openings that both introduce you and mention why you're there.

Family events:

People always seem to forget that their family members know other people. After you get done with the "how's the kids" talk, it's a great chance to mention what you need.

I experienced a great example of meeting people while I was watching my daughter play lacrosse. There I was, sitting next to the same father I always sat near, at another late afternoon lacrosse game. I was one of the "suit" Moms, having just left a client meeting, and he was relaxed in casual clothes. We started to talk, but this time I asked him how he was fortunate enough to make all the games in casual clothes. He laughed and said he didn't feel fortunate. He had been laid off from a great job in a corporate downsizing. The job search was on for him. We began to talk about his talents and skills. Well, two years later he still credits me with having gotten him to begin seeing people differently. Not just as the Mom on the side of the field but as a resource. He is still networking, but now inside a new company where he is very happy. Every time he sees me, he asks what he can do for me. Not a bad benefit from being on the sidelines.

Always
be prepared
to meet
someone.

Easy Practice:

Think of some short introductions for different situations. Practice them in front of a mirror until they sound natural and you're comfortable with them.

Tougher Practice:

Take the introductions you just practiced into the world. Try them out. Track how people respond and if you get the result you want.

Expert Practice:

After you're comfortable with some planned remarks, simplify. Decide what the key words are that you need to get across. When you meet people, vary what you say depending on circumstances, but make sure you get the key words and concepts into your comments.

CHAPTER 13 =
AM I REALLY LIKE THAT?

So there I was, listening to the CEO of a public company telling me how he really cared about his employees. As I listened, I was remembering how he had frozen salaries recently. He'd also cut back on people, eliminating support positions while increasing workloads. I thought about the numerous times I'd heard him screaming at employees about minor things. Being a public company, his salary and benefits were public record. And believe me, the employees knew about every raise he received, all his benefits, and every stock option he was granted or exercised. He couldn't understand why the employees didn't seem to like him better. Perhaps the fact that he never listened, even to the consultant he hired to help him with these issues, had something to do with it.

Now you might be saying to yourself, "Self, what does this story have to do with networking? I think Steve and Kay have gone off the deep end." But think about it. How are you going to understand other people if you don't have an understanding of yourself and the way others see you? The goal of networking is to develop and maintain great relationships with people. It's an interaction between you and them, playing off both your styles.

Years ago, John Grinder, one of the developers of NLP (Neurolinguistic Programming) told Steve that "communication is the response you get." That is, it's your responsibility to ensure that you get your message across to the other person. If they don't get it, it's your fault, not theirs. Now if you both are working at it, so much the better. But when you first meet someone, it's up to you.

> Without self understanding and also understanding how you are perceived, it can be hard to figure out what went wrong when the initial meeting goes bad.

Without self understanding and also understanding how you are perceived, it can be hard to figure out what went wrong when the initial meeting goes bad. For that matter, it's hard to know why it worked if it's successful. As we continue to mention throughout this book, the more you plan and practice the luckier you get about developing chance, or planned, encounters into long term relationships. You need to understand yourself so you can think about, and plan for, what works for you.

Your reputation
precedes you...
make sure it
opens doors
rather than
slams them
in your face.

Remember that there is no right answer.
There's only the answer that works for you.

And it's a whole lot easier to think about what to do and say if you have some idea about your style and how you are perceived. If you find you don't like the way you are perceived, maybe you can even change your reputation through some diligent effort.

If you've been reading closely you might notice we just mentioned reputation. Your reputation is built out of all the encounters people have had with you, good and bad. Over time it becomes a caricature of you, it takes on a life of its own and becomes self-fulfilling as people begin to treat you as the caricature rather than as a person. And most of us fall right into the game. And as we get older we become even more like we are, or are perceived to be.

To be a successful networker you need to have both a good understanding of yourself, and you have to know and manage your reputation. Hopefully both of these things will happen simultaneously as you become more conscious of yourself and your style. There are three things you need to do to address these issues. In addition to whatever general benefit you gain from understanding yourself better, this will also help you become more effective at using the ideas in the rest of this book.

Exercise:

Think about your style. Write down its strong points and its weak points. Do the same for your reputation. What do you like or dislike. Think about how to gradually change those things you dislike and strengthen those things you like.

FIRST THING:

Track what works... and what doesn't. After you meet someone, de-brief with yourself. How did it go? What did I say/do that clicked? What caused their eyes to glaze over? Did I talk too much, too little? What led to them asking me questions? Did I say anything that shut them right up? What did they ask me that got me excited... and what led to their asking me this question? Did this interaction end with a good next step planned? Add whatever else you can think of that will help you do better next time.

SECOND THING:

Self administer a simple behavioral assessment and study the results. Don't get upset or worried at the results. There is no right or wrong. It's just the way you are. It's a tool to help you think about ways to do things better, or differently, to capitalize on your strengths and minimize your weaker areas. Ideally you can get someone who is an expert to discuss the results with you. You might even compare the result to what you wrote down in the exercise above. Do you know yourself well? Are you realistic and honest with yourself?

There are lots of these types of assessment instruments floating around. Steve likes the DISC® forms because they are very simple to use and give you results in plain English... or Spanish... or whatever language you speak. (DISC forms are very simple forms you fill out that give you a simple analysis of your behavioral style.) Kay prefers the Birkman Assessment™, as it allows you to see how you interact with others (such as your work unit) based on their style. It doesn't matter which assessment you use. It's only to give you some information to work with.

THIRD THING:

Ask lots of people you know what they think of you. Tell them that you've been working on improving the way you interact with people and are looking for some advice about how people see you. Some will talk to you, some won't. Some will tell you the truth, some won't. Listen to it all without arguing and then think about it. If you like what you hear, great. If you don't, figure out what you need to change and get moving on it.

Being comfortable with yourself leads to being comfortable with others.

If you can't
be yourself
with someone...
move on.

If you really want to find out this information about yourself, hire an expert to ask people about you and prepare a report with the direction that no comments will be identified. Or do a real 360-degree assessment for yourself just like executives do in the corporate world. Again, there are lots of 360-degree assessments floating around and it's easy to find someone to gather the data for you. (A 360 degree assessment is a personal assessment where people all around you rate you on a variety of factors leading to a composite report where no one is identified so they can be honest about what they say.)

Now you've thought about yourself more than you ever wanted to. You've figured out your strengths and those things where you need a little improvement. You've figured out what people think of you and your style. You've tracked what happens when you meet people, what works well and what doesn't. And now it's time to:

Safe Practice:

Take the best of everything you've just learned and meet yourself in the mirror. Talk to yourself using all your weak points. How do you look and feel? Now try and do the same thing using all your strong points. How do you look and feel? End on this wonderful positive note that you can take into your next networking opportunity.

Not So Safe Practice:

Convince a family member or friend to role-play with you. Practice using all your best skills and ideas. Have them role-play being interested in you, then not being interested. Have them be a tough person to talk to and then a very easy person to talk to. Have them be someone who agrees with you and shares interests and someone with whom you have nothing in common. Play around until no matter what role they attempt, you get them interested in you, until they can't maintain a not interested role.

Really unsafe practice:

Go out into the world and practice on people you randomly meet. See what gets sales clerks, servers in restaurants, or the person next to you on an airplane interested and what sends them running. You never know when sending someone running might be the option you want to use.

Practice in front of a mirror; you only have yourself to bore.

Know

Yourself.

CHAPTER 14 =
I FEEL LIKE A VIRUS

I was on the phone talking to someone who would be attending one of our *Conversation On Networking* shows when the man said "Sometimes I feel like a virus." I immediately said, "Oh, tell me more." I just knew it was going to be interesting. The tale he told was so sad. He would walk into meetings that were for networking and people would walk away from him. He said it made him depressed. I asked him what he did for a living and then I was sorry. Yup, he sold insurance. I instantly knew why people walked away from him — he even tried to sell me and I had called him!

Overselling is an issue for many people. In fact, it often gives networking a bad name. Generally, if you feel you are selling too hard you probably are... unless you are an introvert, in which case you probably can't sell too hard. What is overselling? Well, it depends on what you sell and where you are at the time.

Important Point:
Although we're talking about traditional selling here, remember that we're really talking about all relationship building opportunities. On some level all relationship building is selling. Selling yourself, selling a product, selling a service, even selling someone that they can help you... it's all the same.

So overselling is when you start selling the moment you meet someone, especially when you are not there on a pre-arranged sales call. When you meet someone at an event or a meeting and they say, "What do you do for a living?" it is fine to tell them. Just don't go into the sales mode with your pre-qualification questions. Do make sure you provide a specific answer, "I am a lawyer who helps businesses acquire other businesses" or "I sell residential real estate in the downtown area." Those responses will let the other person know enough to engage you, but won't feel you are being pushy. You may even be pleasantly surprised when they say, "Oh, I have been thinking of moving downtown."

Tip of the Page

If people start taking penicillin when they see you, you have a problem.

Networking is not selling.

**OR** you could avoid being specific in your response and get the other person intrigued. Instead of being a lawyer who helps clients acquire businesses, you could be someone who helps clients succeed at rapid growth. Or as a realtor you could help people realize their dream. Whatever you're comfortable saying that introduces you and gives the other person a chance to enter or leave the conversation at their decision.

But back to the man who "Felt Like a Virus."

> He didn't even ask me about my needs before he began to sell. After my presentation, he wrote a very nice handwritten note to me... except there he was overselling again. The back of the envelope said, "If you know of anyone who needs my service let me know and you will qualify for a gift." When I opened the envelope, out fell his business card...on the back of the card was another offer, "Give me 10 leads and I will pay you $100." He then called to again thank me and ask me for some leads for him. In case you didn't get it, yes, this is overselling. I had talked to him for 10 minutes total, hadn't even bought anything from him, and yet he was aggressively asking me for leads.

As we mentioned earlier, one day we were asked, "How many minutes after I meet someone for the first time do I have to wait to ask them who they use in my business and are they interested in hiring me? And if you're not interested, who can you refer me to." The answer is... if you think these are legitimate questions after a few minutes, you are probably guilty of overselling.

Try this:

Describe what you do in a ten or less word sentence with enough clarity that someone will be able to know whether they need your services. Oh yes, "I am a" count for the first three.

Practice your sentence and the followup of "What do you do?"

Tip of the Page

If you need to ask if enough time has gone by to ask for referrals, it hasn't.

Listen to the other person's answer and ask them about themselves. Since most people like to talk about themselves, if you get them talking they'll find you very interesting. After all, you listened to them talk about their favorite subject. Suddenly their image of you will go up and it is unlikely they will see you "as a virus."

Sometimes we attend consultants' breakfasts or lunches. Our favorites are those where everyone introduces themselves and gets to say three, yes three, words to describe what they do. We always change our words depending on who happens to be there and whether we know many of the people or not. The more we know people, the more esoteric the words become. Some of our three word descriptions are:

Relationships, Connections, Fun

Marketing, Customers, Profits

New Business Development

Creating Lasting Relationships

People, People, People

You know what it is... create several three-word descriptions for yourself. Be creative. Be enigmatic. Be obscure. Be clear and concise. Whatever you say, if you do it well people will ask you what it means and then... you get to talk as long as neccesary to explain what you do.

Well, now you have described what you do in three words, but once you've done that is it all right to ask for referrals and leads or is that overselling?

Absolutely, you can always ask, but doing it at the right time is more likely to produce the results that you want. If you have just sold someone a great new house, it is fine to ask for a referral, but if you just met them it is way too early. Their reputation would be on the line and they don't know how well you do what you do.

The best way to get referrals is by asking clients and friends. Why don't you go through your collection of contacts and give each a Referral Potential Grade of 1, 2, or 3. One means easy to ask and probably will try to help. Two means less easy to ask and might or might not help. Three, of course, means leave them alone until you run out of ones and twos to ask. Now go on and begin asking. Remember that people might move from grade to grade as their and your situation changes. Put new people into a category after you get to know them enough to decide where they fit.

What about stationery, the business cards, the envelope seals? It's the same thing. Figure out the one item that works for you and use it. Just don't over do it — one well placed item is much better than too many and it is unlikely to be viewed by others as over doing it.

It takes
as long as
it takes –
rushing leads to
bruised knees.

Know where it is appropriate to be selling and when it isn't. For example, when I first joined Rotary, I was copied on an email that was sent to everyone in my club. It read in part, "If you don't refinance you house with me, I will have to quit Rotary as I am not getting my value out of the organization." I was shocked. Rotary is a service club. While Rotary is careful to limit the business or professional category to only one member at each club, the goal of the club is not to network to find leads, but to network to develop relationships and perform community service. I never met the person that sent the email. He left our club. I did enjoy the follow up emails from everyone that said how inappropriate it was and that they would never do business with the person. He was overselling, over stepping the boundaries of the organization.

Final thought:

Listen to yourself and watch others when you walk into the room. Do they act like they are glad to see you or act like you are a virus?

Chapter 15 =
Passing the Close...
or Drying up Too Soon

Some people just can't stop talking. For some reason they feel the need to continue to spew information long past the time listeners' interest is over. Then there are the people who turn off their voice long before giving out enough information. It's the same problem driven from opposite directions... there's a close out there somewhere if they could only find it.

So what's a close? In the business world... money. As in, I closed the deal. So why do we use the word close here? We're talking about creating and deepening and maintaining relationships through networking and interpersonal interaction. We think relationships are an ongoing series of mutually beneficial small closes. A relationship develops because things happen that bring fun and delight to both parties. And yes, if it's a business relationship, hopefully some money too.

These small, ongoing closes happen when both people reach the same point at the same time. Mutual agreement to do something. They've closely watched each other and listened to the conversation... sometimes consciously, sometimes subconsciously. They've danced with each other until they came up with something that they agreed about and that led to a next step.

Lots of people are really lousy dancers to the music of networking. They don't seem to watch the effect their words are having. They don't know how to lead or follow without stepping on a lot of toes. Our motor mouth never notices that he's overwhelmed the person he's talking to. Our taciturn woman never notices the continuing lack of comprehension of the person she's talking to. Neither of them ever seems to notice they're dancing to a different rhythm than their conversational partner.

um, so... uh, yes. but...

So then I thought that why not go for the special edition it's only a few hundred more speaking of hundred why don't they make hundred dollar bills in multi-color? I got a multi color sweater at Land Ho for jus 30 bucks or so I remember

Don't drown
your prospect
with a tsunami
of words.

Exercise:

Intently observe the next fifteen people you talk to. Listen to their words, watch their expressions, and make sure you're dancing together.

It's very important to calibrate what goes on around you. When you're asked to lunch, it's a start. When you're asked, "what can you do for me?" it's a clear sign of interest. Answer the question, directly. When someone says, "my business needs help" when they find out what you do, it's an open invitation to tell them how you can help. Be specific.

Remember:

Many of your interactions are small, ongoing negotiations. Whether it's "where should we eat lunch" to "do you like this suit" to "hey, wanna get married," it's all the same. Okay, the importance is different but the process is the same: dance, calibrate and, finally, find a mutually successful outcome.

When Steve was CEO of Workers Transition Network (WTN), he met with the CEO and the Chief of Staff of a division of one of the world's largest insurance companies. Steve was invited for a two-hour session discussing how WTN could help the insurance company. The three of them discussed the WTN service and its financial and customer service implications. The CEO asked his Chief of Staff to work with Steve on a trial project. After about forty-five minutes Steve started to pack up his briefcase. The CEO looked at him and then asked where he was going. Steve replied that he thought the meeting was over but was happy to stay and talk about golf or whatever else was of interest. The CEO laughed and said he was happy to work with someone who knew when the deal was done and appreciated getting back the time to work on other things.

Practice:

Listen for words telling you that it's time for the close, and also for words letting you know more information is required. Try to respond immediately and notice what happens.

More Practice:

Use the words you heard in above practice on others. See which ones are comfortable for you. Watch the effect they have on others and think about how it changes the relationship.

Surreptitious Practice:

Watch other people and figure out if they're dancing together or listening to their own music. How can you tell?

As dancers practice they create fewer bruised feet.

It's a waltz, not a solo performance.

Don't leave your prospect confused by lack of information.

Conversation on Networking

Conversation
on Networking

60

Conversation on Networking:

Now for the Technical Stuff

Now that we've gotten you to the close, we figured we'd better give you some technical advice – so here it comes!

Even though it's supposed to be fun, there are some basic things you have to work at to win.

CHAPTER 16 – NAMETAGS

Nametags are real things, physical objects, versus most of what we talk about. So this leads us into some technical advice. Now don't skip this chapter because of this... we just figured we'd warn you again about this and the following chapters. To keep you amused we thought we'd start off by sharing the story about how Kay discovered a wonderful thing about her parents...

Kay's parents spent many years on the diplomatic circuit in Washington. Her father was a career Army officer. Yes, she is an Army brat but that's a different story. When her parents went to a party they always wore nametags, whether it was at a dressy embassy affair or at a picnic. Her parents always made sure to put them on the upper right chest and sometimes moved Kay's nametag when she put it on the wrong side. Kay figured it was just another one of those Washington things. Then she discovered the truth: her parents actually knew what they were doing. They were wonderful networkers who used their nametags to great effect.

The lesson is...

Nametags bring people together. They allow us all to know each other, even if we never met before. They make people feel more comfortable. No one has to be embarrassed about forgetting names... their neighbor, their supplier, their minister, their distant cousin. We all know it's easier to talk to people if they're comfortable. So why doesn't everyone wear nametags all the time, or at least every time they go somewhere to meet people?

We hear people say they can't read nametags so why bother to wear nametags. Well, if you can't read them, get glasses so you can. It probably means you are also walking by people you should be greeting because you can't figure out who they are quickly enough.

No one complains if you help them identify you.

And, of course, if you are the one making the nametags, make the name large and readable. Use a large font size for the names. In fact, use the largest size that will fit everyone's name on the tag. Don't let artistic creativity get in the way of legibility. Nametags have a serious and important purpose... identification.

 actually met someone recently who refuses to wear a nametag. It seems that this lady wants people to "remember her by her face." Now this is a nice idea, but mostly we keep track of people by their name and other information we can write down somewhere. This is not the time for trying to make people remember your face. Last time we looked, there was no way to send an e-mail via a person's face. Nametags have a real purpose that isn't for you; it's for the other people. Don't let your personal idiosyncrasy get in the way of helping others connect with you. After all, they're still okay, but you've become the loser.

Now here's something really technical for you to look at:

First Name
Last Name

The Name of the Business

So, what if you are wearing that brand new dress for success outfit and don't want sticky gunk on your suit, or even worse, putting a hole in you new silk dress. Have a plan (remember our favorite topic – planning – even with nametags) before you get to the event. Bring a nametag with you to hang around your neck or bring a magnetic one. In fact, you should always carry a nametag with you so that if your name is misspelled or the business name is from two positions ago, you are ready. Not only that, but with your own nametag you can put whatever information on it you'd like to publicize. And don't worry if it looks different from the others, you'll just be more memorable.

Nametags are also a great way to tell who is at an event.

No, not by walking around the room and reading every tag. Instead, arrive early and offer to help organize the nametags on the registration table. Most people organizing a meeting are thrilled with the help and it gives you the chance to read all the nametags. If they're already organized, stand and read them – if someone asks you why, the following are great reasons:

"I'm new to the organization
and I want to see who the members are."

"Last time I was at this event I met some interesting people
and I'm hoping that by reading the nametags I'll remember their names."

"I have been trying to meet some specific people
and I was hoping that they're coming tonight."

"I'm a nametag aficionado."
(What the heck, this ought to at least start a conversation!)

So, does it really matter which shoulder you wear a nametag on? Don't let Kay's mother hear you ask that question. The answer is absolutely. Your right chest/shoulder area allows you to offer your right hand, move your shoulder toward the person and, *POOF!* your name comes magically into view.

Tip of the Page

Carry your own nametag with you.

Wearing your own nametag is a great conversation starter... and your name will always be spelled correctly!

Tip of the Page

Everything you do sends a message.

Everything you do is important to successful networking. It all sends a message. Recently I saw a woman wearing her nametag on her belt, just to the right of where her pants buttoned at the center of her waist. (Yup, Steve is writing this sentence). I won't even speculate about what message she was trying to send.

So when are nametags inappropriate?

The answer is rarely. Sure, you may not need to do it at a family dinner of four, but when you get together at the ten year family reunion and you have the in-laws, not to mention distant cousins from the other side of the world, color coded nametags may even be appropriate to show how the families fit together.

Exercise:

Become a nametag tracker as long as you can stand it. Notice where and how people wear nametags. Notice how many people look at them when they greet someone. Notice what happens if most people have them and a few people don't.

Spooky Exercise:

Make up a few different nametags. Go to some meetings and change nametags during the meeting. Track who notices and who doesn't. Undoubtedly someone will tell you that something about you is different, but they don't know what it is.

Really Odd Thing To Do:

Make up a name to put on your nametag. Go somewhere you never will go again and notice how you feel when people call you by the wrong name. Or wear it where everyone knows you and see what happens.

Final Thought: Even when we are the speakers we wear our nametags... usually our own.

CHAPTER 17 – MAKING BELONGING WORK

Tip of the Page

Know why
you belong.

A former business associate of mine knew I had just started my consulting business and urged me to come to a regional chapter meeting of a women's organization for business owners. She was the newly elected President and "knew it was just right for me." I went to an evening meet and greet where I had a great time speaking with people from a large bank and a local manufacturer. So my friend introduced me to the membership chair who urged me to join. I did right on the spot. The next meeting I went to was not at the same location and the bankers and manufacturers weren't in attendance. In fact, the people there were either sales people trying to sell me their services or people looking for work. Oops, I had failed to remember the rule of three. Attend an organization three times before making the investment to join.

How do you decide what you want to join?

We have emphasized planning in many other chapters, and you certainly need to think about how joining an organization fits your plan before committing to join. Time is a limited commodity and you need to use it well. And, of course, remember that it's all supposed to be fun so make sure it is.

If you can't figure
out why you're
there, quit.

Decide what your objectives are in joining any group:
fellowship, business knowledge, business leads,
community service, peer group...

They are all legitimate but likely lead to different organizations. I had a lawyer client who complained she went to all these meetings and never got leads. So I asked where she went, "...the local chapter of the American Bar Association, Women's Lawyers Group for her firm, and the statewide Women in the Law Organization." I then asked her, "When and why would another lawyer be likely to refer someone to you?" Her mouth dropped open. She hadn't thought about how she only went to lawyer events... and lawyers turn out to be a bad referral source for her.

IF you are looking for fellowship then join a church or an organization that fits your special interests, such as The Hiking Club or Women's Business Executive Golf League. There you will find people that want fellowship and to hike or play golf. Will you ever get a business lead from this group? Perhaps, but it may take awhile. So enjoy the fellowship, the activity, and have a good time. A lawyer I know tracks the length of time from an introduction to getting business, and tells me that five to seven years is quite common.

For business knowledge, you might join the Packaging Managers Association or American Marketing Association (AMA) or Product Development and Marketing Association (PDMA), an Entrepreneur's Forum, or any of the myriad of other special interest business groups. These groups may have networking events and even a networking hour, but your greatest benefit will be keeping current in the field, legally learning about your competitors, and if you ever need a new position, you will know other people in your industry and profession.

So you join the right group.

You have reasonable expectations.

How do you really make belonging work for you?

Get active in the group and demonstrate your ability to deliver on commitments. We know someone who once didn't get a job because the person making the hiring decision had known her as a fellow volunteer. This person failed to deliver on her commitments more than once. Her priority was her paying job. She never thought that not following through in a volunteer position would later haunt her as she looked for a new job.

Take on key roles in the organization.

The Membership Chair can call anyone regarding membership. Be the program chair so that you can demonstrate your creative ability to find interesting speakers and again you can call anyone. Serve as President of the organization so that you are up in front of the membership regularly. Yes, these activities do take time, but if you want to get the most out of what you do, you must contribute.

IN the 1980s I joined a women in business group, eventually serving as Vice President and then President. Now 25 years later, I am regularly in touch with a number of the people I met through that organization. I just finished another consulting project for one person I met there. And yet, I was just looking for fellowship of women in business at the time I joined. In fact, when my employer at that time announced they were being acquired and all the jobs were being relocated elsewhere, it is from the president I served under as vice president that I found my next position. She was now a senior vice president in the human resource area of a local company that was advertising a position in the Wall Street Journal. When I called her, she said, "Oh, that is much too junior of a position for you." I responded "but what if I was unemployed?" I was incredulous at her response; "I'll get the job rewritten so it is right for you. I know you can do a fabulous job and we would be so lucky to have you." Needless to say, the interviews for that position went very well and I had a great five years with that company.

> **Tip of the Page**
>
> If you join a referral lead generation group, remember you are using your good name and reputation to recommend others. Make sure you know, trust and are comfortable with any referrals you make.

If you join,
be active.
After all,
if no one
knows who
you are,
why be there?

Exercise:

Write down the name of every organization that you belong to and list the short term and long term benefits you get from belonging. Then write a goal for each organization for the next year. If you aren't getting benefits and you don't have goals, make sure you have fun when you do go. If you don't even enjoy going, save yourself time and energy, and take a nap instead.

How long do you need to belong to a group before you get leads? The best response is a long time... unless you join an organization that has as its express purpose lead generation. There are plenty of those types of groups hosted by organizations such as Chambers of Commerce or LeTip. As you investigate joining one of these groups make sure the members have the same target audience that you do (business to business or business to consumer).

One last word on expectations:

Realize that it takes time
and investment on your part
to make the most
of any organization,
so be patient.

CHAPTER 18 – BUSINESS CARDS

Tip of the Page

Professional business cards present you as professional. Amateurish business cards... well, guess what they say...

I was standing there having a nice conversation with an old friend, glass of wine in hand. We had run into each other at a professional meeting and were catching up about interesting things that had happened to us since we'd last talked. And then it happened. The dreaded Card Thrust. This gentleman, and I use the term loosely, came roaring up to us, thrust a card at each of us, told us to read it and he'd be right back to talk about himself, and then hurried off to find his next victim. My friend and I looked at each other, decided we were in agreement, and simultaneously performed the Card Hurl... registering two perfect throws into the nearest waste basket.

Everyone has a theory on the best way to use business cards. Some are pretty practical: they make great bookmarks and occasionally win you a free lunch... although if you don't win the lunch you do win a lot of spam and junk mail. Others are hopeful: hand them out everywhere and maybe someone will call you.

And then there's the card itself... the image it creates and the message it sends. The amount of thought and effort that goes into a two inch by three and one half inch piece of paper is phenomenal... except when it's non-existent.

You already know that we believe in planning and preparation as a major key to success. This is especially true for business cards. They are a valuable resource, not to be squandered or used lightly. We even suggest you only hand out cards to people who deserve them, people with whom you're interested in establishing a long-term relationship. It's part of thinking about the purpose of your business cards and treating them with respect. Note: It's all the same for personal cards, perhaps even more so.

What an odd concept: Respecting a little piece of paper.

But think about it.

Treat business cards as a valuable tool for developing relationships.

Before reading any further come up with three or four reasons to respect business cards.

Someone once said that the eyes are the windows to the soul. We think that business cards are the window to the person, or to the company. It's certainly different if you work for your own business than if you work for a huge company. As a matter of fact, if you work for a huge company... unless you're in branding or marketing or some such... you probably can skip the next two paragraphs.

Don't buy cheapo cards over the web or from a quickie printer... unless you want to present yourself and your business as cheap and quick. Your card needs to be well thought out, designed to represent you in the way you'd like to be perceived. It creates a permanent image of you and your business. It can color the way you are seen, treated, paid, and even whether you are hired or not. If you are a great designer, feel free to create your own. If not, please find someone who really understands the issue of image and branding and can create the perfect card to represent the image you desire to present.

Growth Consulting Inc

Kay Keenan
PRESIDENT

1520 North Rodney Street
Wilmington, Delaware 19806

PH 302 777 7969
FX 302 777 7932

KKeenan@GrowthConsultingInc.com
www.GrowthConsultingInc.com

BENARI LTD

POB 197
Birchrunville, PA 19421 USA
Vox: 610-827-7932
Fax: 610-827-7936
ssmolinksy@comcast.net

Steven A. Smolinsky

Philadelphia, Tokyo, Lima, London, Chicago

Not only does your card remind someone about you after you're long gone, they also wind up in the hands of people you've never met. The entire image these people have of you is created by looking at this little piece of paper. Since you are reduced to a two dimensional, two inch by three and one half inch image, it had better be good.

Internal Exercise:

Take out your business card, stare at it intently, and think about the image it presents to the world. Think about if you like this image or not. If not, how would you change it to better represent yourself? If you think it is perfect, congratulations.

External Exercise:

Show your business card to people you know and ask them what it says to them. Try this with people you meet for the first time. Do they tell you what you expect to hear?

SO begin to treat business cards with respect. When someone hands you his or her card, the way you treat it says a lot about the way you think about him or her. Do you simply put it in your pocket without looking at it? Do you make notes on the back while with the person? Afterwards? Do you really look at the card? Do you comment on it? Do you leave it on the table or drop it on the floor?

Each of these says something different. Depending on the situation you might want to do different things. But do it by design and know the effect you are creating. Try to avoid sending the wrong message by accident. If you want to strengthen a new relationship make a few comments about the person's card. Ask a question. If you want to be left alone, ostentatiously drop the card in the trash.

When you really start to look at business cards you'll begin to notice lots of things. Some people only have a phone number or an e-mail address. Some people have six or eight phone numbers. Some cards have a product list; some have the names of several people. Some are printed on both sides or with really dark backgrounds... these people clearly don't understand business cards as notepads. Each of these says something different about the person, the company, what they think is important.

Tip of the Page

Only give cards if you really want someone to call you... otherwise you'll undoubtedly spent time talking to people you wish you'd never met.

If your card
looks like
you're boring,
expect boring
people to call.

Thinking about all this will give you information useful for connecting with people, for understanding them and what might interest them. If they have control over the design, it gives you a window into the way they look at the world. If they have no control, it at least gives you some insight into their company.

Enough about the high level thinking.
Let's talk about some business card basics.

We're always amazed by people who don't have business cards with them. They clearly haven't heard us talk about the fact that every encounter with someone is a great opportunity to expand your horizons. A wonderful fact about business cards is that they are small. You can carry them easily. They fit almost anywhere. Another wonderful thing is that even expensive ones don't cost very much. And they tend to come in these big boxes that hold hundreds. So take them out of the box and place then everywhere. In your wallet, in every pocketbook you own, in the pocket of every suit jacket, in the glove box of your car. And don't forget to keep some in your briefcase.

Now this might seem funny after the previous paragraph on keeping cards immediately accessible, but remember to think about when to give out your card. Having cards when you need them is different than giving one to everybody you meet. Cards are a valuable resource. You need to think about how to use them. We generally wait until we're asked for a card. If someone hands us a card we think about whether to reciprocate. There are situations where we don't want to give our cards to other people... think situations where you know you'll become part of some sales call list. We never put them in the free lunch or other free thing bowls since we already get plenty of junk mail.

How many different cards should you have?
We each have several, since we are part of several different partnerships. We even have some cards that feature us as members of client companies, since we sometimes represent them. Interestingly, we don't have any *Conversation On Networking* cards since while we both view this as a fun-filled and entertaining way to use our expertise while helping our public, we also see it as part of our basic consulting practices. It's a conscious, thought out decision.

This brings us, again,
to one of the key points
of this entire book:

Think and plan in advance. Decide how you want to present yourself through your card and what the outcome of giving someone your card should be. Then design a card to show this image and help achieve this outcome. Use professionals to ensure you do get the best possible result.

Remember:
a key way
someone
remembers you
is from your
business card.

Practice:

Take out a bunch of business cards people have given you and look at them carefully. Note what appeals to you and what doesn't. Think about what image you get from each... fun or boring, rigid or imaginative. Is it a successful card? Do you even remember who gave it to you?

More Practice:

Design your own business card. You don't have to be a great designer, just think about how you want to present yourself and what this requires in a card. If you really get inspired, make yourself a personal card.

Treat business
cards with
respect...
it will rub off
on the way
you treat
their person.

Some More Practice:

Go to an event that includes a card exchange and try different ways of accepting business cards. Watch the different response you get depending on what you do. Really look at some when they are handed to you and ask questions. Stick some immediately in your pocket. Use some as notepads.

Take the results of the above practice and develop several planned responses depending on whether you want to strengthen a relationship or end it.

Japan probably has the most organized business card etiquette in the world. It is formal and structured. I used to go to Japan frequently and discovered that Japanese society is formal and structured. Business card etiquette is a mirror of Japanese society. You always receive a business card when you meet someone. You are expected to hold in both hands and read it carefully. Generally people comment about your card. It helps people understand your proper place in the universe of Japanese society and helps you understand theirs. It shows people that you understand their culture... at least a little. It is not a perfunctory exercise; it is a true showing of respect for the person, the culture, and the person's place in the culture. Be aware of the culture around you and act accordingly.

CHAPTER 19 –
PEOPLE: FOUND, LOST, WHO CARES?

There they sit. Filling up box after box. Staring at me with accusing logos and unused phone numbers, fax numbers, mobile numbers, e-mail addresses, and even US Postal Service or FedEx addresses. Notes that probably once were useful decorate the backs and even fill in the white spaces on the front. Some have yellowed with age. A few have even begun to turn to dust. Any day now I am definitely, positively, for sure going to do something with them.

Some things have a life of their own. Business cards seem to be one of them. We love the fact that in this age of immediate technology one of the best ways of connecting with someone is still to give them a business card. It's really hard to get the same kinesthetic connection through electrons, although we hear you do get a better initial jolt.

Somewhere else in this book we talk about the art of business cards... perhaps the previous chapter. Here we're talking about the art of tracking and keeping in touch... or not. This is the most important decision you need to make after meeting someone, or even after meeting (or e-mailing or calling) them several times. Are you going to continue to make the effort, in time and attention, to continue to develop or maintain this relationship?

This is not an idle question.

Tip of the Page

A wonderful meeting not followed up is like having a winning lottery ticket and not cashing it in.

Sending people
interesting
articles is a great
way to stay in
touch: low key
and thoughtful.

Developing and maintaining relationships is hard work. Steve recently heard from a very good friend. They hadn't talked or communicated in any way in several years. Even though they are good friends and don't even live far from each other, it was just too much work. But it was great fun to meet for drinks and spend the evening catching up. Maybe they'll do it again in a couple of years.

So what can you do about ongoing contact with people you've just met?

They might be interesting. They might be fun. They might be a useful business or life connection. Or they might just be great for ten minutes at a cocktail party.

Exercise:

Think about the last two or three parties – social parties or business events – you attended. How many of the people you met are just good for ten minutes? With how many would you like to stay in touch?

The great thing about this is that you get to decide. It's totally your decision. Even if they call you, you can say that you're really busy for the next three or four years but will be happy to have lunch after that. But with such power comes the need to be ready and able to use it wisely.

These days there are all kinds of electronic ways to track people. It even has a name, Contact Management Software (CMS). How impressive. But notice, it's contacts being tracked, not relationships being developed or maintained. So to be effective and achieve your goal of developing the best relationships for you, there's some thinking you need to do. Then you can enter the electronic age, or not. Many people function quite well with the boxes of cards mentioned at the beginning of this chapter, or even with notes on pads of paper.

Of course, you know by now that we don't think there is one way to proceed. You need to find the one that works best for you. Kay and Steve each use a different system for deciding what to do with people they meet. No reason they should agree about this, since they mostly have different thoughts about everything.

TO START,

You need to categorize your contacts.

Think about who they are, what they do, how much fun are they to talk to, are they interesting enough to displace the time you would spend doing something else instead of talking to them. This last might be the most important. With limited time you need to be cruel in your assessment. If they don't make the cut, send them either to the Never Want To See Again file... sometimes called the circular file...or the Interesting In A Non-Current Kind Of Way file where they can be retrieved at some future time... even though we all know it will probably never happen.

Steve has another system. The cards pile up on his desk and he thinks about them for days, weeks, months and then files as above. Kay makes more rapid decisions. But then they do the same thing. Enter the info in their Contact Management Software. They both happen to use ACT!™. Find which one works for you.

Exercise:

Ask people what system they use and why. Not only will you get some consumer research done, but you also might discover some interesting things about how people decide how to keep in touch with others. It also will tell you a lot about how people think and might give you some insight into how to connect with them.

So, they've passed the test. They enter your Wonderful Enough to Stay in Touch With file. Now what? If you've done this right, you've made a few notes about them. Not only how cute they are, but also useful information about why you want to stay in touch and develop a relationship. Now you need to arbitrage. How much do you want to keep in touch? Are they a must talk to tomorrow, sometime in the next few weeks, every now and then, once a year?

Tip of the Page

Have a system – a pile of business cards, a bunch of sticky notes, a slick, web-based contact management system – whatever works for you.

NO matter what the case, you do need to follow up immediately just to cement the meeting. These days an e-mail will do. A hand-written note is usually nicer. Both should say the same thing. "I enjoyed meeting you yesterday. Isn't it interesting that we both have poisonous toads? Look forward to seeing you again."

To be able to properly take advantage of people you meet, you need to know something about them. Business cards are great little notepads. We suggest writing: where/when you met the person, what you discussed, identifying a memory aid like the person is very tall, follow-up discussed, anything else of interest. Since it is a small space, it does help you boil it all down to the essentials.

Otherwise, what you do will depend on your follow-up routine. And even that can be automated these days, but you have to get the information into your system. And put in the appropriate follow-up as a reminder. And read the to-dos every day. And most important... do them.

This last is where most folk fail. They've figured out with whom they want to connect. They figured out how. They've done all the data input and record keeping. And then they just don't have the time. Well, we suggest that you don't have the choice to not have the time. It should be part of your weekly calendar, just like lunch, the gym, reading e-mail, and even doing your job. Give up one hour of soap operas a week in return for developing your life.

And, did I mention this? Plan how to proceed with everyone you meet. Remember, as you internalize this you will become great at rapid decisions about where to throw that business card. Few will make the preferred list, but those that do will lead to great things.

Practice:

Carry a pen or pencil with you, so you can immediately make notes on cards you are given. Try doing this while still talking to the person and try doing this after they leave. Notice the difference in what you write and they way the treat you. It's ok to write 'Circular File,' but not while they are looking.

Masochistic Practice:

Go through some old cards. See if you remember who the people are and where you met them. Decide why you bother to save the cards. The card of anyone where you don't have a clue can be used as kindling.

Time Management Practice:

Dedicate a set time each day/week to use strictly for follow-up. Make sure some of this time is used to catch up with folk you used to like but have lost touch with.

Writing Practice:

Randomly send some people e-mails and some people note cards as follow-up to initial meetings. Track which methods work best for you.

It's really hard to stay in touch with lots of people... be selective.

Everyone has his or her own method of follow-up. The other day I found a message on my phone from a person that I know professionally. She said, "Your business card just fell out of my Rolodex™, so I knew I had to call you." I called her back partly to see if she really still uses a Rolodex (she says she does), and because it was nice to know that she was thinking of me.

Chapter 20 =
Surviving Trade Shows and Conventions

I went to a meeting the other day. There was a big convention in town and I got a free pass so I figured I'd go and meet some people. When I got there I was overwhelmed. I didn't realize that there would be thousands of people wandering around, hundreds of booths, and numerous lunches and speeches and seminars. So I walked around randomly. I never did get to any lunches or speeches or seminars. I did manage to run into several people I know. We mostly talked about how huge the event was and how overwhelmed we were. The best part is that I came away with a bunch of stuff... lots of squeeze toys, candy, pens, water bottles...

Ever been to this convention? I see lots of hands raised. What a horrible experience. We've all done it. We've gone to a place... not necessarily a trade show... where we think we can find lots of good information and meet lots of new people only to be overwhelmed. We come back with a bag full of junk and without having connected with anyone. Or only having connected with someone trying to sell us something we don't want.

We've been on both sides of the convention/trade show booth.

For those of you who haven't ever worked a trade show, it can be even worse than being an attendee. All of those people walking by and you have no idea which ones are decision-makers. And if you do talk to someone, how do you figure out whether they're someone worth keeping in touch with or only someone looking for free candy.

The answer to the question "how can I have a successful convention or trade show" is the same whichever side of the booth you're on. Determine your desired outcome and do the appropriate planning as well as preparation. It's amazing how many people show up, on both sides of the booth, without doing any preparation other than getting dressed that morning.

Although there is certainly some art to successfully negotiating a trade show, there's plenty that relies on planning and preparation. The first task is to figure out why you're going.

There are good reasons and bad reasons.

Bad reasons:

- If I don't go, I'll just have to work in the office.

- I hear they give away lots of cool stuff.

- I always wanted to go to San Francisco (well, maybe this one isn't so bad).

Good reasons:

- I want to see what the leaders in providing services to my industry are doing.

- I'd like to meet some thought leaders in my field and hear what they have to say.

- All the prospects I want to meet will be there.

It really doesn't matter what the reason is, as long as you know what it is so you can decide what are the criteria for success. Here's the critical idea: If you know how you'll know you've been successful, you can plan what to do to achieve this success. If you have no idea why you're going and what success would be, stay home.

So preparation is the key.

Get the floor plan, attendee list, and exhibitor list... whatever information is available. Study this information. This doesn't mean taking a quick look and then throwing it all in a folder never to be seen again. Read it all, make notes, and figure out who are the important people to meet and the best companies to visit. Lay out a plan for meeting all these people. Great networkers and connectors set up lots of appointments in advance... even with people they've never met. After all, the reason people go to these shows is to meet other people. Take advantage of it.

Tip of the Page

If you go to an event with someone, split up. It improves your chances of meeting someone interesting (we like this so much we used it twice).

Don't gather
lots of stuff
at trade shows...
successful people
already have
their own pens
and Post It™
notes.

So now you're there.

It's time to think about logistics. You're planning a military operation: the most effective way to achieve the objective with minimal loss of life. In this case, remember that the life you have to lose is yours... makes you want to plan a little better, doesn't it?

If we continue to think about this like we're planning a military maneuver, what's the first step? Reconnoiter the terrain. It might be a small space or a huge convention center. The process is the same. Take a quick walk through. Notice where the people are you want to meet. Notice if there's anyone else there who looks interesting. Add them to your list. Think about how much time you have and plan accordingly. Remember that there are slow times when booth workers are desperate for people to talk to.

Now this is going to sound so obvious that I hesitate to mention it, but... visit the most important people you want to meet first. You'd be surprised how often we hear "I really wanted to meet Fred, but just never got around to it." If you really want to meet someone, plan to make it happen. Afterwards you can spend time collecting trinkets.

Have your most important questions ready...
whichever side of the booth you're on.

It's not a random process. With opportunities to meet people everywhere, you need to make good use of your time. Have two or three questions ready to use to quickly decide if you want to hang around or move on to the next person. It's really easy to get stuck for hours with one person who you really didn't want to know in the first place.

Remember, you don't need to meet everyone. What's important is that you make two or three good connections... or even one if it's the right one.

Although the above sounds like it's for those attending the show, it's the same for those working the booths. Why are you there? Who would you like to meet? Did you set up appointments with prospects in advance? Did you check out who else has a booth? How will you know if it was a successful event? And the most difficult, what's you plan for following up?

Jerk detachment: if all else fails just leave; they'll never notice.

And when you leave the real work starts.

Actually following up with all the interesting people and prospects you've met. But that's in other chapters.

Practice:

Next trade show or convention you attend, make sure you get the exhibitor and speaker list in advance. Go through them carefully. Decide in what order you want to visit the booths. Figure out where to be to insure you meet the speakers you want to meet. Prepare a question or comment for each speaker so you actually get their attention when you introduce yourself. (Of course, you can do this last piece at any event where there are speakers.)

Difficult Practice:

Go to a local trade show for something of interest but for which you have never attended. Get the exhibitor list in advance and note which ones look like they might be interesting. How many interesting people do you meet that you'd like to talk to again?

Fun Practice:

Go to the State Fair and use the same planning discipline and see how much more fun you have.

Tip
of the
Page

Trade show
success
takes work –
plan before
you go.

Steve went to a trade show not too long ago. He's on the board of a voice recognition software company – Fastlane Construction Software, in case you're interested. Because Steve is such a connector, the CEO asked him to go and see if he could find some new customers or strategic partners. So he put together a list with the help of the CEO and off Steve went. The show turned out to be huge. It filled the entire Atlanta Convention Center. After meeting all the people that the CEO was interested in, Steve decided to visit the rest of the show.

But where to start? Should I look at the sparkling construction vehicles and other equipment? The little boy in me pointed this way. Should I wander randomly for exercise if nothing else? Actually using my own advice, I started at one end of the show – booth 9386 – and then proceeded to walk through every aisle taking a quick look at every booth. It took several hours to do this. At the end, there were four booths that had caught my attention, three for the CEO and one for myself. Returning to these booths – a story in itself – I wound up with a couple more good contacts for the CEO and one for myself, which led to a consulting project.

Know your outcome
and plan how to achieve it.

CHAPTER 21 = GOLF... OR NOT

Tip of the Page

I actually have a client who was a golf pro for thirteen years. Then he decided to get a job like the rest of us, so he became a financial planner. At the first company he worked for, they told him not to take advantage of the fact that he was a golf pro. They were so rigid that they couldn't understand the marketing value of his past. So he went elsewhere. Now, he and I have a great time developing odd and unusual (of course, since I'm involved) ways to take advantage of his expertise. And he's doing quite well with quirky messages about lowering your score while building your bank account.

Any activity can be a great networking opportunity.

Now why start a chapter called 'Golf... or Not' with a golf success story?

Because it's an interesting story that shows how you can use your past to create success in the future. And it lets you know that we do realize that golf can help you meet people, especially in the business world. But this story could have been about any special knowledge or expertise you have. You don't have to play golf to be successful... in business or in life... no matter what some people tell you..

We are often asked how to build business relationships when you don't play golf. Generally, the question is posed as a statement "Everyone else in my firm plays golf to entertain prospects or clients, but I'm not a golfer."

Our first response used to be "Why don't you play golf?" Then one of Kay's clients told us how she went to a week-long tennis camp with her spouse. She came back feeling good enough about her tennis game to be comfortable playing with other people. Then she joined a tennis club for experience as well as fun. She now plays "customer tennis" and is enjoying the sun, fun, relaxation, and her business is booming! Now we ask, "What do you do that connects with other people?"

Tip
of the
Page

Inviting can
be as useful as
doing.

Golf isn't for everyone. A lawyer we know regularly tells everyone in earshot that he hates golf. Yet, he will always volunteer at a client's or favorite non-profit's golf tournament. A number of years ago he was flipping hamburgers at just such an event when a partner of another law firm approached. In casual conversation, the golfer mentioned that my friend had been the topic of conversation as the golfer's law firm was trying to fill a position. While flipping hamburgers, my friend mentioned he might be interested in talking further. He is now a partner at that firm.

> There's lots of ways to take advantage of things you don't do or even particularly like. If it's the place to be, figure out what you can do so you'll have fun and get to meet some people.

Here are ten alternatives to golf to consider.

There are certainly hundreds or thousands or maybe even millions of such things, find what works for you. Our guess is that most people have never been invited to these types of activities as part of building a relationship.

1. **Visit a museum, followed by lunch in the museum café.** This is especially wonderful if there is a special exhibit and you can get a docent dedicated to your party... even if it's only for a party of two.

2. **Charter a boat and sail while you eat picnic-style.** Remember to first ask if people get seasick.

3. **Offer a pair of tickets to the ballet or to a theater company.** Even if they hate dance and theater, they'll remember your offer. Might even remember it more if they do hate these things.

4. **Use your camera constantly as a visual diary.** At events – social gatherings, business meetings (when appropriate) – wherever you can, take photos. Put the best ones in handsome paper matte folios, and give them to people. Remember that humor is great, but embarrassment is deadly. You never know when you'll see them on someone's desk or find out they've told people all about you.

5. Play tennis, or horseshoes, anything that helps develop a relationship. You can even invite multiple people to join in.

6. Attend afternoon tea. For the right person, afternoon tea is a terrific form of entertainment. A bit different, soothing, and conducive to discussion during the late afternoon. And yes, men like this too... although they might not admit it at first.

7. Take people fly-fishing. If you don't have a great spot and lots of gear, hire a guide who will also provide you with the necessary equipment. Or take people duck hunting... with a camera. Anyone can enjoy this without the need to worry about shooting anything, or anyone. And the pictures can be displayed without offending anyone.

8. Attend a minor league baseball game. Get box seats and include children. There will be a lot less people and a lot more entertainment than at a major league game.

9. Take them to a cooking class with you. What better way to develop a relationship than chopping vegetables and burning sauces?

10. Host a wine tasting. Get a wine store or restaurant to help you. Supply some great appetizers. No, don't get them so loaded they forget they were there.

And a bonus one:

11. Just ask them to go for a walk with you. Around the block is fine. It clears the head, calms the nerves, and gives you a chance to talk.

And when all else fails,
take them to breakfast
at a diner.

The worst that will happen is they'll say, "no."

Tip of the Page

Try something different.

What do you like to do? How can you use this as a networking opportunity? Try it and see what happens.

Exercise:

When you do the above activities on your own, or when you do whatever you enjoy, turn it into a networking opportunity. Really talk to the person in the next seat, or the waiter, or the person in line behind you.

THINK OUTSIDE THE BOX

Note: Kay wrote an article on this topic originally published by the American Bar Association. She offers special thanks to the members of the Delaware Forum of Executive Women for contributing their proven options to the original article.

CHAPTER 22 = KEEPING IN TOUCH

If you forget them, they'll forget you.

With cell phones, PDAs, PDAs that are cell phones, cell phones that are cameras... and send pictures instantly, instant access to e-mail, why would we write a chapter on Keeping in Touch? Because often when we're talking to people who are suddenly thrown into a situation where they need to network, we hear "Oh, if I only had stayed in touch."

> I was with the head of personnel at a very large company who said it well: "I get so annoyed when people that knew me fifteen years ago call and act like we are still close friends. They haven't needed me or been around to offer assistance when I needed it and now they have their hand out to me." We discussed if she gets annoyed at all the calls or only some. She reflected for awhile and said, "Oh no, the people that admit up front that they need something and say they realize it has been a long time are fine callers."

There are a couple of messages here.

Keep in touch. You never know when you'll need a favor or a job. If you forget this message, be upfront about having made a mistake. It's okay to make mistakes, we all do. The cover up is what always gets you, just as in politics.

Good networkers don't only go to meetings. They keep in touch with lots of people. There are plenty of different ways to keep in touch. Here are a few we especially like.

It may be obvious, but *you really do need a good contact management system.* And you need to learn how to make it work. If you're technologically challenged as Steve is, don't get nervous. Your system can be as basic as a Rolodex™ holding business cards combined with a paper calendar. Or it can be a sophisticated electronic system like Outlook™ or Act!™. What's important is that you have a system and use it... every day.

Keep in touch...
you might find
you inherited
something.

Your system needs to be where you are and full of information to be most effective. Use it to make notes about the people you meet – spouse and children's name, former jobs, or where they went to school are all tidbits that help. Use the calendar to remind you about dates, make followup phone calls or send someone an e-mail, or, even better, send a note by real mail. And when the time rolls around to send that e-mail, do it.

If you only use an electronic device, stop right now and back it up. It's your networking brain and if you lose it you die. Sort of like what happens if you lose your head. Then back it up continuously, automatically, if possible, since otherwise it rarely gets done. The nice thing about electronic systems is that if it gets stolen, lost or goes for a swim... and you backed up continuously... you can replicate it. For those of you using paper systems, it's a lot harder to make a copy, but try to do something anyway.

> **If you only use an electronic device, stop right now and back it up.**

Real mail – remember this stuff?

Letters and note cards have almost disappeared – no one gets real mail anymore. So it really stands out when you use it... and it shows you put some effort into staying in touch, not to mention spending money on stamps and cards. Recently, I went to Alaska on a Holland America cruise. I took a roll of postage stamps with me and sent one hundred postcards. No, not all to family, but very deliberately to former clients, current prospects' gatekeepers who I have gotten to know, administrative staff at existing clients and my best referral sources. I sent only a hundred because the ship ran out of free postcards. Yup, they're free for the asking. Cruise lines ...and many other places...know about how to network... through their customers.

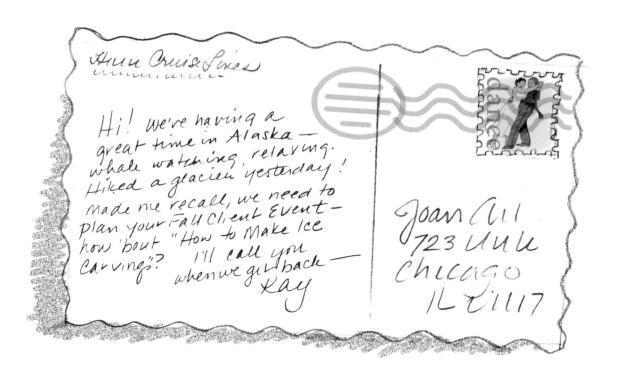

Hu... Cruise Lines

Hi! We're having a great time in Alaska — whale watching, relaxing. Hiked a glacier yesterday! Made me recall, we need to plan your Fall Client Event — how 'bout "How to Make Ice Carvings"? I'll call you when we get back —
Kay

Joan Cul
723 Uuu
Chicago
IL 61117

Before I returned home the postcards had begun to arrive. My phone was ringing when I walked in the door. I made sure that the post-vacation slump was avoided by spending twenty minutes a day for five days on keeping in touch. Fun and easy to do. Months later, people are still mentioning getting the postcard from Alaska. Oh, one other thing, let me say it again, all the postcards were free – some from our hotels and others from the cruise ship.

Exercise:

Send out a bunch of postcards next time you go somewhere. There are even restaurants with postcards, so you don't have to go far to try this out.

Tip of the Page

Postcards are small... you don't have to say much.

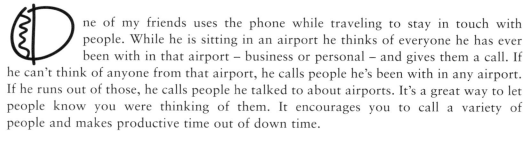
Holey newspapers are another great way to stay in touch. Using them tells people you're thinking of them. So what are holey newspapers you ask? It's the reason I get my local newspaper. It is not a global newspaper, but is full of stories about people I know. I cut out any article that mentions their name, their kids, their business or something we have spoken about. Then I paperclip a little "thought you'd be interested" or "thanks for working for the community" note to it written on the back of my business card. I hand address the front of the envelope and stick it in the mail. Have I ever gotten work because of one of these notes? One call about some work came from a long time acquaintance a week after sending him a clipping. I had been keeping in touch with him for four years because he was someone I enjoyed, he worked for a good company, and he always asked me about my business. That clipping closed the deal.

Exercise:

Send out a dozen newspaper articles and see what happens.

One of my friends uses the phone while traveling to stay in touch with people. While he is sitting in an airport he thinks of everyone he has ever been with in that airport – business or personal – and gives them a call. If he can't think of anyone from that airport, he calls people he's been with in any airport. If he runs out of those, he calls people he talked to about airports. It's a great way to let people know you were thinking of them. It encourages you to call a variety of people and makes productive time out of down time.

Although it's hard to plan, even sending e-mails to the wrong person can be a great way to keep in touch. We know someone who was doing a poor job of keeping in touch with past clients. As you all probably know, assuming you do a good job at whatever you do, past clients are generally a good source of future work. One day this fellow called to tell us of his great success with a former client. It happened because he accidentally sent a project update to the former client instead of the name above it in his email address book. As soon as he realized the error, he tried to retrieve the e-mail but discovered it had already been opened. So he picked up the phone to explain. The former client said, "Oh, I'm glad you called. We have work we need to have done and I was just wondering who to call when your e-mail arrived. It made me decide to add you to the list of prospective suppliers, but now that you're on the phone – I'll just give it to you." How to make an OOPS work in your favor, and even better – this fellow learned the lesson. He started to call his former clients, just to say hi.

Most people use Christmas cards as an annual way to stay in touch. They show up in the mail with lots of other cards, and at a time when no one is paying attention. Send New Year's postcards that go out sometime in January. They'll arrive all by themselves and catch people's attention. Or send them in March or June. It reduces the stress for you. After all, you can do them whenever and wherever you want...like in front of the fireplace at a nice ski resort. And best of all, they provide an entertaining break for whoever gets them. And they will remember you and the card. It's just like the cruise postcards. You'll hear from people that love having gotten them and talk about how they break through the clutter. How about sending Valentines... "We love getting referrals from you, thanks."

Exercise:

Yup, you know what it is. Send a few cards according to the above suggestions or use your own ideas. And, of course, see what happens.

As hard as it is to believe, some people do all of these things and more. Some people do some of them and have their own special additions to our list. Some people do none of these, but have their own ways of keeping in touch. Whatever they do, all these people share something: they are great networkers with a huge collection of ongoing relationships. What will you do now?

Exercise:

Pick up the phone and call a few people you haven't talked to in quite some time.

Relationships develop over time and through keeping in touch.

Conversation on Networking:

And now for some final thoughts...

Conversation
on Networking

CHAPTER 23 – IMPROVE DAILY

Be flexible.

Becoming an expert networker and relationship builder is like anything else: it takes practice. It's like that saying I mentioned before, "the more I practice the luckier I get." The nice thing about developing and maintaining relationships is that the practice is easy, you can do it anytime and anywhere and no one will even notice you're practicing on them. And you should practice all the time and everywhere you go.

We've listed a few things that you can do every single day. In an amazingly short time they will become so ingrained in your daily activities that you'll even forget you're doing them. Remember, these are our ideas for some simple ways to keep yourself tuned up to be a successful networker. Start with them, but expand them by including ideas from the rest of this book, by trying what seems to work for other people, and by creating your very own personal ways to improve your skill.

There is no single right way.

Let me repeat this:
There is no single right way.

There are lots of ideas floating around out there in the world. Give them a try, but always remember that the right way is what works for you. Your gut is never wrong. Butterflies in your stomach are your body revving up to be successful. But if it feels really bad, try something else. It's hard to make a good impression while fighting with your insides.

Have fun,
be fun and
enjoy life.

So here are some things to do every single day:

✔ Smile at yourself in the mirror first thing. Remember, smile not grimace.

✔ While looking in the mirror, practice an introduction of yourself.
If you don't want to meet you after hearing it, keep working on it.

✔ Think about the new and exciting thing you're going to tell people who ask
"What's New." Tell it to everyone from the bus driver to your boss.

✔ Send someone a handwritten note. Do it for no particular reason.

✔ Practice listening.

✔ Be positive. Try to spend the entire day without once saying anything negative.

✔ Clip an article and send it to someone who might be interested in seeing it.

✔ Ask for a referral or introduction to someone you'd like to meet.
Offer something in return.

✔ Change some aspect of your daily routine: something different for breakfast,
invite someone you hardly know to lunch, go to a movie that you'd never go to
before we told you to do this, read a magazine that you didn't know even
existed.

✔ Call someone you haven't spoken with in a long time.

✔ Leave everyone you meet in a more pleasant state than you find them.

✔ Remember that you are a great person who knows things that are interesting,
unusual, and unique.

Plan, plan, plan.

Prepare, prepare, prepare.

Practice, practice, practice.

It's a process, keep it going..........................